GLENN PATTERSON

LAPSED PROTESTANT

NEW
ISLAND

Lapsed Protestant
First published 2006
by New Island
2 Brookside
Dundrum Road
Dublin 14
www.newisland.ie

© Glenn Patterson 2006

The author has asserted his moral rights.

ISBN 1 905494 24 6

British Library Cataloguing in Publication Data. A CIP catalogue record for this book is available from the British Library.

Cover photograph © Jim Maginn www.jimmaginn.com
Printed in the UK by CPD, Ebbw Vale, Wales

New Island received financial assistance from The Arts Council
(An Chomhairle Ealaíon), Dublin, Ireland

10 9 8 7 6 5 4 3 2 1

CONTENTS

Welcome to Northern Ireland	I
I am one of the people …	9
As others see us	12
29/12	15
Orange culture	20
Hope and glory	23
The true embodiment	27
Just like him	29
House	39
Accommodation and apartmentality	44
Muggins	50
Murals	53
Kerbstones	62
Open up	66
Stranger here myself	71
The Hewitt	78
Linen Hall	83
Peace pause	87
Take two (three, four, five…)	90
Belfast to Boston	93
Be(lfa)st boy	98
Stand up for the Ulstermen	I06

Billy bhoy 110
Cigs 116
The people's army loves the people 120
Ask me another one 123
McCartney sisters 127
D.I.O. 132
Love poetry, the RUC and me 135
The BBC made me a deconstructionist
(and called it macaroni) 144
It could be anyone 146
Never-ending stories 158
Traffic 164
Homelands 173
Out of myself 186
Christmas 1994 189
Afterword 194

Welcome to Northern Ireland

A guide for New Millennium tourists

A

Assembly. After decades of resistance to rule from Stormont on the one side and power-sharing on the other, we now have a Stormont Assembly with a power-sharing executive. The high ratio of Assembly Members to population (108 of them for 1.5 million of us) was intended to ensure that none of the 'parties who have previously predicted the mood of' this or that paramilitary group were excluded. And still the UFF-predicting Ulster Democratic Party couldn't get in.

Adams, Gerry. President of Sinn Féin, architect of the northern republican strategy from the 70s on. Not to be confused with the other Gerry Adams, named by many authors as a senior figure in the Provisional IRA and who disappeared some time around 1981.

B

Bloody Sunday. Long, long overdue enquiry soon to be underway, despite the efforts of the *Daily Telegraph* and elements of the British military. Some would like this to be the cornerstone of a Truth Commission, though it remains to be seen whether, say, a Provisional IRA leader who disappeared around 1981 would be any more willing to talk about Bloody Friday than the Paras are to talk about Bloody Sunday.

Bellaghy, birthplace of Seamus Heaney. Think bog, think blackberries, think Bethlehem, to American academics. Think Big Tourist Bucks. Good man yourself, Seamus.

Bann, the River, to the east and west of which Northern Ireland is said to divide. (See 'Portadown'.)

C

Crack, the. Alcohol-, rather than coke-based fun; what we were all supposed to be sustained by when times were toughest, as in 'Ach, I know the place is bombed to fuck, but we can still have a bit of crack.' With luck, the last victim of the Troubles.

Communities. A polite term for sides. There are apparently only two, though where this leaves the Chinese community, the Indian community, the Gay community, etc. is anybody's guess. (See 'traditions'.)

Crown, the. A bar. The island's finest. Survived countless bombings only to have its famous stained glass windows smashed this summer by two drunks wielding chairs.

Citybus. Formerly 'the red bus'. Much-improved Belfast service, now that half the fleet isn't burned out every second week. Also operates a controversial 'Troubles tour'.

D

Drugs. Don't bring with you on your Citybus Troubles tour, unless you want to become part of a living history 'punishment beating' demonstration.

Derry. The centre of its own universe. Also known as Londonderry, the outpost of somebody else's.

E

Eden. Village outside Carrickfergus. Famous for its Eden Says No graffiti. Like a good many other places, Eden will need to have something new to say for itself, and fast.

Everyone knows. Northern Irish for 'our party thinks'.

ER or *Early Release*, a programme about which, here as elsewhere, opinion is sharply divided. Finale scheduled for June when the last prisoner will walk from the Maze. A proposed second series, *ER - The Exiles Return* (expulsions by paramilitaries have carried on unabated into the ceasefires), has so far had a lukewarm reception, not least from some of the biggest fans of *ER1*.

F

FT_, universal graffiti, which roughly translates 'you are now entering... '. The third letter, P or Q, for Pope or Queen, will tell you whether you are in a Protestant or Catholic area.

Fence. The place where all those who did not subscribe to the orthodoxies of nationalism and unionism were said to have been sitting all these years. Surprisingly commodious, in my experience, and heavily populated.

G

Giant's Causeway, the. Genuinely impressive volcanic rock formation, though rumours that it predates the rhetoric of the Democratic Unionist Party are surely far-fetched.

H

Homer. DJ David Holmes. Our U2. Famous enough now to be the subject of the Jesus Christ joke. (What's the difference between X and Jesus Christ? Jesus Christ doesn't walk around town thinking he's X.)

I

IRA. Once there were two, Provos and Stickies, now available in three exciting new varieties: Continuity, linked to Republican Sinn Féin, Real, linked to the 32 Counties' Movement, and, for the image conscious, I-Can't-Believe-It's-Not-IRA, a.k.a. Sinn Féin. (Patrick Kielty ate my punchline!)
IPLO. A splinter of a splinter of a splinter group. Another split or two should get rid of the last three letters entirely.

J

Jesus Christ. According to some evangelical Protestants would have voted No in the 1998 referendum. Famous enough to appear in a David Holmes joke.

K

Kylie. A popular forename among thirteen-year-old girls. (The original memorably accompanied Nick Cave at the 1998 Belfast Festival.) More power to them, and the Jasons and the Lees. Who's going to tell me any of these are 'Protestant' or 'Catholic' names?

L

Lambeg drums. Almost always a misnomer. True Lambegs often require two people to carry them. Bass drums are what most bands feature. The sound is duller and less rhythmic than the Lambeg's, and consequently much more unnerving. *Loyalist fringe groups.* Scarier than a thousand bass drums. Fundamentalist enemies of 'left-leaning' Progressive Unionist Party and all things Catholic.

M

Murals. Wall paintings with all the grace and charm of giant tea-towels. 'Folk art', according to some. 'The cat's piss on the corner', according to political commentator Malachi O'Doherty.

N

Northern Ireland. That (not Ulster, the Province, the Six Counties, or the North) is the name, don't wear it out. *Never, never, never.* DUP-speak for 'not until we get the departments we want and competitive ministerial salaries'.

O

Orangemen. Very few wear bowler hats, still fewer actual sashes. Collarettes over double-breasted navy or brown suits seem to be the norm. Temperance lodges tend to be on the small side. *Opening hours.* Originally relaxed to combat the attraction of paramilitary-run drinking clubs, now longer than anywhere else in the United Kingdom. Some change you effected, you guys.

P

Paisley, Rev. Ian, a political institution.

Purdysburn, a mental institution.

(Try to keep these last two separate in your mind. Try harder than that.)

Portadown. The river Bann runs through it. More importantly, the train does too.

Q

Queen. God save *our*. (Sung *fortississimo*.)

R

Royal Ulster Constabulary. Variously the finest body of men and women in the known world and the paramilitary arm of the Unionist party. Proposed name change to be resisted by five-year-olds who will otherwise be deprived of their only joke: 'Why are the police called the police? Because they R, U C.'

Residents' groups. Spontaneous manifestations of local resentment to Orange parades. No, honestly.

S

Socialism. Our natural state, it seems. We're so good at it, nobody needs to practise it, least of all those parties who claim to espouse it.

Sainsbury's. The place to hie to in the event that it all goes horribly wrong. As last in, the large supermarkets are a fair bet to be first out. Expect helicopter airlifts from their roofs.

T

Total abstinence lodge. Two auld fellas with a banner.

Traditions. As for communities, though may also refer to dancing with your arms by your side and/or marching around in a collarette.

U

Union of Catholic, Protestant and Dissenter. Legacy of the United Irishmen and what most of us would claim we are trying to achieve. Stunning lead in this taken annually when the Gaelic Athletic Association votes to continue its ban on members of the security forces, past or present.

V

Victory. Nobody had one. Which explains all that racing around in cars, a couple of years back, with flags and scarves flapping out the windows.

W

West Belfast. An area that extends further south than much of south Belfast and excludes from its purview some of the westernmost, inconveniently Protestant, districts of the city. Annual festival, in the spirit of inclusiveness, organised to coincide with Internment commemorations. Mind you, Internment? Inclusiveness?

Waterfront Hall. Flagship of the new Belfast. 'The People's Palace', so-called by everyone bar the People.

War, the. The preferred term for a grubby murder campaign, indulged in with varying degrees of sophistication and accountability by republicans, loyalists, police and troops. Often referred to still, more than three decades after it started, as 'the last twenty-five years'.

X

In the old scheme of British Film classification, generally marked the spot under which the Free Presbyterians would be standing singing hymns and waving placards. More recently they were to be found outside an all-male production of *Romeo & Juliet*, and the Gilbert and George retrospective at the Ormeau Baths Gallery – to the obvious delight of Gilbert and George.

Y

'yes I said yes I will Yes'. James Joyce, *Ulysses*, from the David Trimble Book of Helpful Quotations, the manuscript of which has been ready for some time, though publication has been repeatedly put back. Now expected February.

Z

Zeds. After thirty years of tumbling out of bed for the first news bulletin of the morning, and sitting up till all hours for the last bulletin of the night, what most people here will be catching once the Assembly is in full session.

Observer, January 2000

I am one of the people...

I am one of the three hundred and twenty million people
living in the states of Europe joined (pre-Nice Treaty) in
economic and political union. I am one of the sixty million
people living on the islands immediately west of the
European peninsula; one of the six million people on the
smaller of these islands, of the one-point-five million who
inhabit the six north-easternmost counties of the historic
nine-county province of Ulster that make up the adminis-
trative region of the United Kingdom known as Northern
Ireland.

I am one of the countless thousands of people who left
here in the 1970s and 1980s hoping to make a life across
the water free from crap about Protestant and Catholic,
Orange and Green, about what school you went to and what
street you lived in; one of the very many who found the first
thing they had to do upon arrival at the other side was

explain themselves to police officers in terms of what street they lived in, what school they went to …

I am one of the people who returned eventually. Who knows why?

I am one of the people, numbers strictly anecdotal, who use Across the Water and not The Mainland when referring to the larger of these islands and These Islands to avoid the potentially offensive *British* Isles. I am one of the people who will likewise avoid saying Ulster or the Province on the one hand and the North, the Six Counties or Failed Political Entity on the other.

I am one of the people with a British passport who could equally carry an Irish one and have considered it often, if only in hopes of better treatment in the event of a hijacking somewhere in the Middle East; one of the people who feel perfectly at home in England, but will cheer on almost any country in the world playing England at football. I am one of the smaller group of people who will not mind England victories if Manchester United players score the winning goal and am, incidentally, one of the people who could name more players from Bayern, Barcelona, possibly even Bruges than from the Belfast teams competing in the abysmal Irish League.

I am one of the three hundred people who turned up, in pairs, on Saturday, 12 May 2001 to the failed attempt at the world record for couples kissing simultaneously (we were six hundred couples short) in Belfast's Odyssey arena, a mile from where, late on the night of Friday, 11 May, three Australian tourists were beaten so badly one of them required plastic surgery to his ear. Orange bastards, their attackers called them. What did they think, those were *Protestant* accents?

I am one of the people who voted for the Good Friday Agreement, aimed at bringing peace and stability to Northern Ireland, and one of the ones who worry that the Agreement has made this a more divided place than ever to live in.

I am one of the two people who will get out of bed to feed Marvin and Daisy Blur the cats in the morning.

Correction: I am the only person.

Identity Papers, Brussels 2001

As others see us

'The problem with Ireland is the English.'

I'm standing on a street in Boston while a woman I've never met before holds forth on what ails this place.

'The Protestants aren't real Irish. They leave, it'll all be OK.'

The woman knows where I am from, she just assumes that, being where I am from, I am what she thinks I am. She's a pleasant woman, she's laughing a lot. She believes what she's saying is making me feel good. I'm wondering whether to tell her that I am, by designation if nothing else, a Protestant. But I'm in no position to stop her. I did ask her, after all, what she thought of Northern Ireland, and her entire monologue is being filmed by the man standing next to me, David Barker.

I have spent a significant part of the last six months in David's company asking relative or complete strangers the question I asked the woman on Boston's Newbury Street. Fortunately, for the documentaries we were making, a surprising number of these people — from Massachusetts to Macroom, Islington to Arkansas — took the trouble to give their opinion.

Or maybe you don't find that so surprising. We Northern Irish are used to being looked at. We are among the most scrutinised people on earth. (I have a vivid memory of me and my friends, aged eleven, finding a Swedish camera crew outside our school gates. 'Look, a Swedish camera crew,' we said, much as we might have said, 'Look, two dogs sniffing each other's bums': it was worthy of remark, but there was something seriously wrong with you if you paid it too much attention.) I've often wondered, though, whether we aren't too busy clamouring to broadcast our own particular version of the truth to listen to what others are really saying about us.

Much of what I heard while making the series surprised me, quite a bit amused me, and some, I have to say, made me blush. At times, the experience was how I always imagined it would be overhearing a conversation about yourself when the other guests thought you had already left the party.

Did you know, for instance, that our plumbing appals newcomers to these shores? (Or did you, like me, think that nowhere in the world was it possible to drink water from the cold tap in the bathroom?) Were you aware that, despite our old-fashioned attitudes to sex, there are men on the London gay scene who *only* sleep with men from here?

Some of the qualities we pride ourselves on do appear to have a basis in fact — we *are* unusually friendly, to outsiders at any rate. Our much-vaunted sense of humour, on the other hand, gave at least one interviewee a severe pain in the neck.

Gerry Adams is our best-known politician. The Ku Klux Klan admires him. The KKK admires the IRA. The Orange Order baffles most outsiders. Our idea of a salad baffles not a few.

That's the way the conversations went. A Vietnamese-American who had talked earnestly about the international consciousness of those involved in 'the struggle' laughed suddenly in exasperation as she told how, after a week among them, she wanted to get a T-shirt printed: *I AM NOT CHINESE*. A recent arrival, a Norwegian, illustrated her thoughts on identity by referring to her support for Glentoran. 'There's a good atmosphere in the Oval,' she said.

The only rule David and I set ourselves was to avoid politicians. Actors, we talked to, television psychiatrists, journalists, restaurateurs, students, tour guides, we talked to. We talked to immigrants and emigrants, visitors and people too scared to set foot here.

And at the end of the six months of listening to them — six months which have witnessed some of the worst instances of intolerance and brutality in our intolerant and brutal history — all I can say is we are lucky so many people seem genuinely to care. Care as much about our schoolgirls, sent out in winter in short skirts and knee socks, as about how we will manage to live together in the future. I only wish I agreed we were always worth the bother.

Belfast Telegraph, November 1998

29 / 12

Huge yellow gobs spatter the quivering window of white on the living room wall, then gradually dissolve into the close-up smiling faces of two toddlers, who sit, side by side on a kerb, waving plastic Union Jacks. Behind them are two rows of adults (one seated, one standing), more flags, a dense privet and a pair of pre-war semis backing on to a valley. In front of them is a broad road, which is beginning to fill with marching men, some with flutes, some with drums (though the only sound in the room is the whirr of the projector), others carrying swords and wearing fringed sashes. And bobbing along in their wake, an orange ribbon ('sash' would be overstating it) draped from collarbone to hipbone, is me, aged thirteen. Twelfthing.

At the very moment that I (as was) arrive centre frame, I hesitate slightly and glance over my shoulder and I (as am) freeze the film, looking back at myself looking back.

Thirteen, therefore my fourteenth Twelfth, though only the sixth that I can attach a year to with confidence, for it was not until a month after my eighth that I heard gunfire in the night and became rooted in time. A couple of miles away, at the source of that sound, people were dying, among them a boy not much older than I was, shot while sheltering in his bedroom. I read of their deaths the following day in the *Belfast Telegraph* – my first recollection too of seeing the name of my city. The next Twelfth, my ninth, the army was on duty along the route of the Belfast parade. One soldier lifted me up into his ferret car, parked at the bottom of Finaghy Road South, and I watched from behind its protective armour as the bands and lodges wheeled right, off the Lisburn Road, over the railway bridge to Finaghy field. Being eight and new to the subject I not unnaturally ascribed historical significance to the choice of destination and thought Finaghy must be a very important place. The year after that, though, the parade went instead to Edenderry and all future thoughts of 'over the bridge' were dominated by what lay at the top of Finaghy Road North, Andersonstown. (The old field was eventually converted into sports grounds, or, as it was indignantly reported south of the bridge, *Gaelic pitches*.) Shortly after my thirteenth birthday I caught the train home to Finaghy from Lisburn baths. The station name had been obliterated by graffiti: 'Fuck the Queen', 'Up the Provos'. Half a dozen boys my own age or slightly older watched from the top of the bridge as I climbed the steps from the platform. I was so scared I couldn't speak when they asked me what I was. Very considerately they asked me just to point to where I lived. I pointed south. They lived north. They kicked my lights in.

'It'll harden you,' my friends said, 'taking the train.'

The next Eleventh night, drunk on lager stockpiled through June ('Mister, mister, go into the offie for us. Aw, mister, go on, just one can. Thanks, mister...'), I cruised the bonfires looking for Twelfth kisses. The Eleventh night exceeded even New Year's Eve in its potential for licence. I succeeded in lumbering (a long-forgotten word that captures the technique perfectly) one girl who let me squeeze my hand down the front of her high-waister trousers. I kept it there, motionless, for five minutes before finally withdrawing it. I don't know which of us was more relieved.

Needless to say my hand didn't stay still when I bragged about it to my friends the next day, the day I walked with the men for the first time.

My father was standing with his home-movie camera at the roundabout below Barnett's Park. He filmed two toddlers grinning and waving plastic Union Jacks while he waited for the procession to appear. And he filmed me as I passed by, looking back over my shoulder.

I have caught up with myself. The projector whirrs on, my head jerks round again and I continue across the living room wall, facing forward.

I never did walk with a lodge again, though in subsequent years I followed this band or that (the Kick-the-Pope the better) to the field. On my seventeenth Twelfth, which was not, in fact, on the twelfth at all, I followed one band I knew as it made its way between skyscrapers and shopping malls to a pedestrian precinct in downtown Toronto. (There are at least three Twelfths that I know of besides the *Twelfth* Twelfth: the Wee, the Scottish and the Canadian – something to do, perhaps, with the *Twelfth* Twelfth's own migration from the first of July. Indeed I would not be surprised to learn that there are as many different Twelfth dates as there are countries with Orange lodges to observe them.) I had sat my O Levels the previous June and was in Canada visiting relatives. I attended socials in a Rangers Club cum Band Hall west of Toronto and heard 'The Protestant Boys' sung in the bug-crackling darkness of late-night poolside parties. One émigré Orangeman I met told me how he'd laid out some dumbfuck Canadian with the mace once for attempting to cross the road during a parade:

'Bastard nearly broke the ranks,' he said.

I suppose it was the vastness of Canada that made this belligerence over a matter of feet sound so absurd to me at the time, so *irrelevant*. But, of course, I was wrong. Nothing could have been more relevant. For if the essence of the Twelfth is not contained in the destination of the march (take your pick, Belmont, Finaghy, Edenderry, Toronto), nor, ultimately, in its actual date, then it can only lie in the act of marching itself. The Twelfth is the march and the march is the demonstration of nothing so much as the ability to march when and where the marchers please. The medium is the message and must remain inviolate.

Though I trace the roots of my disaffection back to that summer in Canada, I did not formulate these thoughts until a couple of Twelfths later, my twentieth (held on the thirteenth, a Monday, as if to prove the point about dates, though ostensibly to keep the Sabbath holy), when, trying to reach a friend's house in the University area, I found myself walking down the Lisburn Road away from town as the parade and its followers were walking up it. It was the summer of the hunger strike (indeed a prisoner had died that very morning) and the ranks were even closer than usual. I had never before felt myself to be so conspicuously out of step, nor experienced such hostility in my own city.

'If you aren't walking with us,' the looks said, 'you must be against us.' And I understood then something of the psychological threat Catholic friends had talked of feeling when they heard the pounding of Orange drums. (Green drums are equally terrifying, but they of course are kept well away from the city centre.) When I finally reached my friend's house I was shaking with fear.

The next Twelfth I spent with my girlfriend in a cinema in Dublin and the Twelfth after that again I was in England, for good, or so I told myself.

Yet here I am, back in Belfast, running home movies of Twelfths past. A band crosses the living room wall. Friends of mine half a lifetime ago. I would have been walking beside them that day if I hadn't been such a tube on the flute, for despite months of practice I only ever mastered two tunes: 'The Queen' and 'The Billy Boys'. There has been much talk lately of emphasising the folk festival aspect of the Twelfth, restoring the carnival atmosphere of 'the old days before the Troubles' (a reference no doubt to the fun-filled folk festivals of 1857, 1864, 1872, etc., or the famous York Street carnival of 1935). The suspicion of the minority community, this argument runs, is based on a misunderstanding of what is really being celebrated. But there is no ambiguity in a song like 'The Billy Boys': 'We're up to our necks in Fenian blood, surrender or you'll die.' The truth of the matter is, of course, that the Twelfth has never aspired to ecumenism and no amount of tercentennial revisionism can disguise the fact that the Orange Order has its origins not in the 1690s but in the bitter sectarian warfare of a century later. The Twelfth is by its very nature divisive and, in its embolic, intrinsically militaristic progress through the streets of Northern Ireland, it is an annual reminder of the power of the past to mobilise and paralyse in one.

Orange culture

I won't lie, I would really rather I wasn't writing this. I would really rather not be thinking about the Orange Order at all just now. As a Protestant-born writer, I feel I have been asked to comment on Orangeism and its rituals once too often already. I have written about my one experience of walking on the Twelfth, aged thirteen, about building bonfires, getting drunk and yelling, shamefully, fuck the pope; I have written about the moment when I found myself literally walking against the Orange tide. I have often written what I think will be my last word on the subject.

Like many another thing here, however, the subject does not go away; as surely as the marching season comes around, comes the offer to comment again. The slant this year is Orange 'culture'. I suspect a great many people when asked about Orange culture would reply, adapting Gandhi, that it would be an excellent idea; in fact, though, the word 'culture' has been so devalued in Northern Ireland as to be practically worthless. 'Culture', I find, nearly always carries a lot of 'side'. 'Culture' too often, and perversely, is our sick-note out of self-examination and change. (Are you reading, GAA?)

It is time the Orange Order stopped being disingenuous. The Twelfth demonstration and the three thousand smaller parades are not folk festivals capable of being enjoyed by all sections of the community. The fact that some Catholics do not take exception to the parades, might even come out to watch them (as several of my Catholic friends did the last year I watched the Twelfth), does not give the lie to this. The Orange order *is* hostile to Catholicism and Catholicism cannot be distinguished from the individuals who follow it. (Which is not the same thing as saying that all expressions of Orangeism are, or need be, hostile, or that its primary purpose is to give offence.) The Orange Order ought to admit, too, that it is does not represent *Protestants*, but a version of Protestantism, which, despite the lodges and parades in other countries, is still an essentially Northern Irish version. In fact, substantial though the Order's membership is, in terms of the population as a whole, Protestant and Catholic, Orangeism in Northern Ireland is a minority interest. Which is not the least of the reasons why its rights — since that essentially is what the culture debate is all about — have to be defended.

There must be honesty all round. I don't doubt for a second that residents' groups are composed in the main of people genuinely concerned about the disruption caused by Orange marches. (And I am mindful that the behaviour of some bands and their followers, and of some Orangemen themselves, has not, in the past, tended to make their presence more acceptable.) There are others, though, for whom thwarting the Orange Order is an end in itself. The message that residents too have rights is as important as it is obvious, but couching this message in rhetoric which is inappropriate to the circumstances is, to say the least, unhelpful. The Orangemen's insistence on walking is not a case of 'croppies lie down'; nor is the Orange Order, however much one may dislike it, the Ku Klux Klan.

And I am certain that in saying this I will be accused by some of a lingering Orange bias. It seems to me, however, that where rights are concerned we must apply ourselves not to the most obviously defensible (i.e. our own), but the least: the rights of people wholly unlike us and with whom we are least likely to agree. If we were *all* to look out for each other's rights we might at last begin to get somewhere; to a position, say, where residents insisted on the loyal orders' right to march only for the loyal orders to insist on the residents' right not to be inconvenienced by unwanted parades. Of course, there might be a few heated exchanges as the parties disputed which should bow to the other's generosity, but finally, I am sure, they would allow one another the right peaceably to disagree.

A real culture of political maturity exists where people, believing themselves to be right, have the courage and confidence to allow others to think they are.

Fortnight, July 1998

Hope and glory

Last Friday I finished an essay on the state of Northern
Ireland in the wake of the IRA pledge to dump arms. Last
Saturday, I got a new fridge. Bosch frost-free. It arrived
earlier than expected. The old frost-free-for-all fridge still
had to be chiselled out of its ice block and cleaned to go
into the garage. The garage still had to be cleared to accom-
modate the fridge. I may be gone some time, I told my wife,
arming myself with the portable stereo and a couple of –
sadly alphabetised – CDs: The Warlocks, present-day
twenty-something psychedelic throwbacks; and War fea-
turing Eric Burdon, the genuine freak-era article. When they
were exhausted I tuned to Radio Five Live, Manchester
United squandering a one-goal lead against arch rivals City.
Fearful of a repeat of 1974, when City won and United
fans lit fires on the Stretford End, I switched to the local
station.

Which was when I discovered I hadn't spent the afternoon in the garage at all, but a Tardis. I had travelled back beyond Denis Law's back-heel, beyond War's wig-outs. An Orange march had been rerouted and Belfast had erupted – our own main road had erupted – like it was 1969.

I don't know if you are familiar with the person of Garden Centre Prod. He lives in affluent north Down and, as his name suggests, has better things to do than bother with the politics of this place, still less vote. There are no lengths I *wouldn't* go to to vote, but – call me Garage-Clearing Prod – this city would not have been in the state it was in on Sunday morning if a few more Prods had done *anything* other than run around the streets on Saturday afternoon.

Two summers ago the climax of the marching season, the Twelfth of July, fell on a Saturday. Belfast City Council organised a weekend of events, including a classical music concert in the city's Botanic Gardens. Whether the intention was to dilute the Orangeness of the parade, or to build a broader cultural festival around it, most people were agreed, it was one of the least tense Twelfths in living memory. Least tense *and* sunniest. The day of the concert I was in – well, guess – buying a patio umbrella, when I bumped into Danny Morrison, writer and former publicity director of Sinn Féin. I think he may have been buying a barbecue. I think I may have said, so it's true, *all* shades of political opinion here are moving towards the garden centre.

There was, as it happens, alfresco music in Belfast again last Saturday night: the newly traditional nationwide link-up to the Last Night of the Proms. The venue this time was outside the City Hall, where we Belfast people go to welcome in the New Year, wave at American presidents, protest against their wars in the Middle East, or – all-too-regularly over the years – to protest against the killing of our own citizens by our own citizens.

My wife and I switched on the TV looking for news of what was happening a mile down the road and found the Proms overrunning. 'Land of Hope and Glory' was being sung, in the Albert Hall, in Cardiff, Glasgow, Birmingham and Manchester. But not, apparently, in Belfast. We watched through 'Jerusalem', 'The Queen', 'Auld Lang Syne'. No Belfast. Given the roadblocks around the City Hall earlier in the day, given the helicopters we could hear clattering overhead, it seemed possible the concert had been called off.

It hadn't been. Belfast had simply opted out of the ending. The BBC says it was a matter of running times. A friend who goes every year says she can *never* remember Belfast screening those last few anthems and voices the suspicion that this was another instance of our fear here of giving offence, or of our refusal to countenance being offended.

If Garden Centre Prod means nothing to you, you are probably equally unfamiliar with the late James Young – a sort of Belfast Dick Emery, if you can apply that to your own scale of what is and isn't funny. Young's LPs were very popular in our house when I was a child. On one is a song called 'Me Da', about an ageing Orangeman, whose shoes are polished and whose collarette is ironed before every Twelfth of July.

Like many of Young's characters he is a sentimental creation and one who seems separated by more than just the passage of time from the Orangemen who folded their collarettes on Saturday before hurling stones at the police. At one point in the song, the old man finds himself in a

Dublin cinema, standing to attention while the Irish National Anthem is played. When his son asks him why he stood he says, Ach, I just imagined it was 'The Queen' playing instead.

It seems that in 2005 we are incapable even of this parsimonious politeness. So, whatever the reason, no 'Queen' for us on Saturday night, no 'Jerusalem' and – thanks to the antics elsewhere in the city of those who might have been expected to sing the words loudest – no glory, and not a lot of hope.

Night Waves, September 2005

The true embodiment

In the early summer of 1973, with a murder rate in Northern Ireland of roughly one a day and a bombing rate in Belfast, it sometimes felt, of closer to one an hour, my primary school decided to mount a production of Gilbert and Sullivan's *Iolanthe* in which, for reasons which take three acts and innumerable songs to explain, a conflict erupts between the House of Lords and the Kingdom of the Fairies.

I sang 'O, Little Town of Bethlehem' at the audition ('but in thy dark streets shi-i-i-i-neth the everlasting light...') and landed myself the lead role of Lord Chancellor. Not long before, Dustin Hoffman, then thirty-two, had been aged to look a hundred and twenty-one in Arthur Penn's *Little Big Man*. Finaghy Primary School's teachers set their sights a little lower, ageing an eleven-year-old by a mere fifty years. But then, Penn had the legendary Dick Smith and a Hollywood effects budget to call on. Finaghy Primary had a few sticks of greasepaint. Still, the audience watched, awed by the transformation – or so I always remembered it – as old-man-me marched on to the stage to sing, 'The law is the true embodiment of everything that's excellent, it has no kinds of faults or flaws and I, my Lords, embody the law.'

I could sing it for you now. I could sing all the other characters' songs too. In fact, I did sing all the other characters' songs back then, or at least mouthed them, in between singing my own. Why not? I was having the time of my life up there. (In a touch worthy of Gilbert and Sullivan themselves I had fallen in love with the girl playing the boy with whom the girl who was my ward was in love.) The finale had us all, Lords and Fairies, singing it's love that makes the world go round and flying off to Fairyland.

Recently I found a photo of the leads, standing in the school playground. There is the girl playing the boy who is loved by the girl who is my ward, and there I am, at the centre, a chubby eleven-year-old with tinfoil buckles on my black gutties and purple and white lines on my face; and there at our backs is the school fence and beyond it who knows what manner of early summer '73 mayhem.

The Vacuum, September 2004

Just like him

I am not, I don't think, a bad person. Certainly not in that glamorous 'mad and dangerous to know' way. Nevertheless, I have done many things in my life which I would consider less than good; things of which I am not proud, even ashamed. Some years ago I behaved badly to someone with whom I had been in love. We had been living together for almost a decade. I met someone else and fell in love with her. I left the woman I had been living with. I left England where I had been living with her. I returned to Belfast to look for a place to live with my new love. The circumstances were shoddy, yet in my heart I knew that what I was doing was right. Right for me, right for the person I had come back to Ireland to be with. For a few weeks, while I searched for a flat (my lover had not yet moved from her home in Cork), I stayed with my parents, in the housing estate where I had lived until going across the water to university.

My parents were trying very hard to understand why I had ended my relationship in England. They had been fond of my partner, loved her like the daughter-in-law which in law she was not. They were trying hard to love me as their son the same way they had loved me before they knew I was unfaithful and hurtful.

It was late spring. My parents went out for frequent walks. I spent a lot of time in the back garden, smoking. I was in the house alone one night when there came a knock at the door. Two men stood on the doorstep. I remembered them both from my youth, though I hadn't seen either of them for a good many years. I remembered them as loyalists, hard men. They remembered me.

'Glenda,' one of them said.

Glenda is what some of the people on my estate began calling me when I came home for my first summer vacation from university. I had taken to wearing nail varnish while I was away, dyeing my hair and crimping it. I had taken to wearing tight black leggings and carrying a shoulder bag (handbag, these people preferred to think of it as), sometimes black, sometimes pink. I kept my hairspray in it.

Of course, back then, their ridicule didn't bother me. I invited it. Their ridicule was a measure of the difference between us and I was determined to be as different as I could possibly be from the people I had left behind.

By the time I returned to live with my parents I had published two novels. I had written articles and made television documentaries in many of which I had been critical of the values and beliefs of my Ulster Protestant background. My hair may no longer have been crimped, but I had succeeded in becoming someone completely other than the person I had been when these men and I were teenagers together.

'Glenda. How's it going?'

There were, I noticed, looking out from the hallway, other men at other doors in my parents' street. They all had collecting tins. I had been away from home for a long time, but not so long that I had forgotten what door-to-door collections in spring were for.

'Do you want to give something for the new band uniforms?'

The band was our local flute band. They had the reputation of being loud and aggressive: 'blood and thunder' is the old-fashioned term; 'kick the Pope' they would be called today.

Every year before the Orange marching season began, members of bands would go round the doors asking for money. Uniforms, was what they usually said, though I didn't know too many people who asked to see proof of purchase.

It was part of who I had become that I did not like Orange marches or flute bands. It was part of who I had become that I accused those who turned out to watch them of condoning and perpetuating sectarianism. Mostly, though, I had been proclaiming this all-new me while living away from Belfast.

I was feeling a little vulnerable that spring. The woman I had fallen in love with and who was coming to Belfast to live with me was from south of the border. I was not sure as yet where we would end up having to live. I couldn't guarantee that I wouldn't be seeing a lot more of our local band.

So when the men rattled their collecting tin again, I went in to the living room of my parents' house and found my wallet.

'My dad would probably have given you something if he was in,' I said as I dropped a pound coin into the tin.

Of all the things that I did in those weeks, that is the worst, the one I am most ashamed of.

When my parents returned some time later I told them what had happened.

'I wouldn't have given them a penny,' my father said.

As I knew he would.

The night my mother met him, New Year's Eve 1951, she heard his friends call him the Big Wheel.

She knew he was from the market town of Lisburn, she knew his surname was Patterson. She knew there was a department store in Lisburn, J.C. Patterson's. Lisburn, Patterson, the Big Wheel. It all added up very nicely.

In fact, my father's father – though also J.C. – was a linen worker. He had named his son after his own brother, Phares. Pronounced Ferris. As in the fairground wheel.

By the time the pun dawned on my mother, it was too late. She was smitten.

My mother's name is Nessie. Short for Agnes. (She had an aunt called Agnes and the choice, if she was to be distinguished from her in conversation, was between Aggie and Nessie, and Aggie, to the child my mother was, was too old a name.) Like my father's, my mother's is not a name you hear every day. Nessies, I imagine, must dream of a John or a David to absorb a little of their strangeness; Phareses of a Mary or an Anne. But this Nessie and Phares found one another.

They were married in Canada. My mother's parents had emigrated there, six months after she and my father met. My mother had intended to stay at home, but when her younger brother fell sick shortly after arriving in Canada, she went out to join the rest of her family. My father at once gave up his job and followed her.

This was the beginning of the 1950s. For a young man like my father, it must have seemed as though there would always be jobs, wherever he went; but, still, giving up the job he had on an impulse was, as they say here, just like him.

When he was fourteen and old enough to leave school, he had been offered a job at the BBC radio transmitter outside Lisburn: a glorified tea boy, but even in those early days of broadcasting, even without hindsight, surely an exciting opportunity, a foot in the door. My father turned down the job and went back to school after the summer vacation in order to be eligible for the Northern Ireland schoolboys' football trials. He had good cause for thinking he might make the squad: an uncle, who played semi-professionally in the Irish League, told me recently my father was the best left-sided player he had ever seen. He made the last-but-one cut. The final trial, though, did not go well. (The day got off to an inauspicious start. The trialists had been sent the shirts they were to wear in advance. One of the selectors complained about the state of my father's. 'It looks like you slept in it,' he said. Which was exactly what my father had done. Well, he explained to me, he'd never had a proper football shirt before.) He left school immediately on hearing he had not been selected for the schoolboys' squad. The vacancy at the BBC had been filled, of course. Instead, my father was apprenticed as a sheet metal worker to the Ulster Transport Authority, at the bus depot overlooked by Lisburn Central, his old school.

In Canada he worked in a textiles' factory and played amateur football for Galt Celtic, a team made up of recent Irish immigrants. Opposing teams included English immigrants (Hespler Hotspur) and Italian (Internazionale of Guelph). He was known to his team-mates as Pat Patterson. He and my mother had three sons in a little under four years. This being North America, they had, for young married people, a good life. But my father was homesick. His relatives in Lisburn sent him reel-to-reel tapes of family singsongs: sentimental standards, for the most part, 'The Mountains of Mourne', 'That Little Old Mud Cabin on the Hill'.

Possibly against my mother's wishes, my parents came back to Belfast in the final months of the 1950s. They thought they would like to have an Irish girl to go with their three Canadian boys. So they tried for another baby, and they got me. Glenda.

My father was back in work again within days of his return home. He had a spell in the shipyard, where the last of the great Belfast liners, the *Canberra*, was under construction, and then moved to an electronics firm in the east of the city. (These were the days when computers were the size of small houses and were built by sheet metal workers.) A short time after he started in this job, one of his colleagues was sacked for taking time off to get married. The work-force went on strike to get the colleague reinstated. The dispute made the Belfast papers. The Honeymoon Strike, it was dubbed. My mother told me not long ago that she and my father, with four young sons, were hit so hard by that strike that for years afterwards they were, financially speaking, running to stand still.

I don't know how the strike ended, but whether or not the colleague got his old job back he was soon in another, better one. I remember visiting him and his wife when I was still quite young in their new bungalow in Belfast's northern suburbs. If I think of the Sixties, in fact, the Sixties as aspired to rather than the Sixties as they were lived by most in our provincial city, the Sixties distinct from the violence that came at the end of them, I most often think of that bungalow and the couple who owned it.

I believe they left Belfast soon after the Troubles began.

My father then was thirty-seven, the age I am today.

My father and I are father and son, which is to say we are close without knowing very much about one another. We talk about events, rather than emotions. We keep from each other certain of our hopes and fears and doubts. I have never, for instance, asked my father whether he has dwelt on the direction his life might have taken if at certain moments he had made certain other choices. (That my being here to want to ask him is dependent upon the choices he did make is not, of course, lost on me.) Whatever, while my father was still in his thirties he found himself, with a million and a half of his fellows, living in what was in all but name a civil war.

As a person who came to full consciousness *in media res* I try often to imagine what it must be like to be faced with such a situation. What, in the previous course of your life, prepares you for arriving, as my father did, at the scene of a bomb blast close to your brother's place of work and seeing what you suppose, from the colour of the hair, to be your brother lying in the road, only to find that you are cradling the remains of a woman?

I have, in my fiction, returned to this question repeatedly. It has occurred to me recently that I have written a lot about my father.

Some of my father's other friends left Belfast in those early years of the unrest. One friend, Joe, took his family to Boston after his teenage son came under pressure to involve himself in street violence. Joe's family and my own lived a mile apart, in estates, lying at either end of an east-west aligned road, which were mirror images of each other. Joe's estate, like Joe and his family, was, according to the only definition that seemed to matter any more, Catholic; our estate was Protestant.

In both places, at the turn of the Seventies, there sprang up vigilante groups. (At the time I thought the term a Belfast invention.) The fear in those days was of mobile squads of gunmen, touring the night-time streets. My father took his turn with the rest of our adult male neighbours and stood at the entrance of the estate after dark on the lookout for suspicious cars.

Perhaps he only did this for a matter of weeks, perhaps it was many months. (I was, you have to remember, asleep while all of this activity was going on.) What is certain is that he ceased as soon as he realised that the moment for ad-hoc, unarmed vigilante groups was about to be overtaken.

Some time in the summer of 1972, the Ulster Defence Association began drilling on the playing fields of our estate. The UDA was a paramilitary organisation which had its origins as an umbrella organisation for vigilante groups. They appeared to me, a child watching them, to be composed of a younger element than the original vigilantes. They wore uniforms of denim jackets and bush hats, jeans and Dr Marten boots. Many wore hankies over the lower half of their faces. Undoubtedly, as with the IRA, there were still men in the UDA's ranks who were much like my father. Men who had taken the decision, however, based on what they understood or believed of the circumstances of that time, to go a step further than vigilantism. As with the IRA, a good many went a good deal further in the years that followed.

No longer merely 'Protestant', ours became known as a 'UDA' area. Drinking clubs in the locality (and, with night-life in the city centre close to non-existent, all localities had them) were referred to as UDA clubs, since it was generally assumed that takings from the bar and the slot machines went to fund the organisation. There were other ways of funding. Protection money, like vigilantism, was another term I thought we Northern Irish had invented.

It must have been autumn 1972 when the UDA came collecting door to door on our estate. The rumour preceded them: windows were being broken in houses whose occupants refused to donate. Like all the best rumours, this one had the virtue of plausibility. Even a passing acquaintance with the news confirmed that broken windows were the very least that might, at that stage of the 1970s, befall a person not supporting the cause.

As I recall it, the whole family – my mother, my father, my three brothers and I – were in our sitting room (which, with a settee and two armchairs, sat only five) when the knock came at our door. My father went to answer it.

I am a fiction writer, so perhaps I do not actually remember my mother – when my father returned – her voice troubled, saying, 'Oh, Phares.'

He hadn't made a donation. But neither that night, nor the next, nor any of the nights that followed were our windows smashed.

I am not, as I said, a particularly bad man. My father, by the same token, is perhaps not an exceptionally good one, not a man without shortcomings and contradictions. His refusal to donate was a small act. (And I have no way of knowing how many other households responded in the same way.) Its significance, though, lies in the fact that, even at that time of extreme polarisation, it denied the legitimacy of claims that organisations like the UDA spoke for 'their community'. Without the validation of people like my father, their community could only ever be the community of those who actively or tacitly supported them. It left a space between religion – an accident of birth – and political belief.

The very space I have tried all my adult life to live and work in.

By the way, it would be just like my father not to remember that I contributed to the flute band, that spring evening in 1994, on the pretence of believing that he would have done so had he been at home.

My father would probably say it is just like me *to* remember and, remembering, to make such a big deal of it: what's past is past, he'd say, and there is no point dwelling on what cannot be changed.

Soon after that night, I found a small house for rent in the University area. I got the keys on May Day, the day before Ali, my new partner, the woman whom, in the abstract, my parents were opposed to, was to arrive in Belfast. My father and mother insisted on helping me clean the place from top to bottom. They were still there when I left to meet Ali off the train, but were gone an hour later when the taxi dropped us off at the front door. They had bought flowers, to make the place more welcoming for her.

And that, finally, is so like the two of them.

New Writing 9, 2000

House

In April 1994, after several years living in Manchester, I spent the evening at a friend's house off Belfast's Antrim Road. The house was a late-nineteenth-century three-storey townhouse on a tree-lined avenue. My friend, a photographer, showed me his ground-floor office, his top-floor dark room, his long back garden. I asked him what he had paid for the house. He told me. I whistled as well as I was able to after an evening drinking wine. 'I want to live here,' I said. 'No,' my friend said, 'you don't. It's too Catholic for you. It's too Catholic for *me*, and I'm a Catholic.'

The next day I travelled to Dublin to meet the person on whose account I was in Ireland at all that April. I had first met Ali while writer-in-residence in her hometown university of Cork. She was ready to leave Cork; from the moment we met I wasn't going back to Manchester. We talked about Dublin, halfway from everywhere (I know Dublin, I know, you're a great place in your own right), before deciding to give Belfast a go together. I could see we might have a bit of a problem finding a place to live. Infuriatingly, for two people who practised no religion, what was not 'too Catholic' for me could well be 'too Protestant' for Ali. There had always been mixed areas in Belfast, by no means all of them middle class. North, south, east and west in the post-war years, integrated housing estates were built on the edge of the old, divided Victorian city. I had grown up in one such estate, Erinvale, in south Belfast. Even while I was in primary school, though, I was aware that housing could be a contentious issue. Some of the earliest Civil Rights protests were to highlight discrimination in the allocation of local authority houses. As tensions mounted through the 1960s and into the 1970s, the question of who lived where became literally a burning one. In my own estate, several Catholic families were pressurised into leaving, to be replaced by Protestant families who had found they were no longer welcome in the estates where they had been living.

By 1994, the safest bet for the mixed or mixed-minded was in a half-mile radius around the university, taking in the Lisburn Road, the Stranmillis Road and (unlikely as it might sound) the so-called Holy Land, off the Ormeau Road, whose streets were named for places in the biblical Middle East. These were small terraced houses at suburban semi prices. Ali and I could rent here for a while but not afford to buy. All too soon we were thrown back on the 'too Catholic' or 'too Protestant' conundrum. Ali scoured the property pages with an outsider's eye. 'Look at this,' she'd say. '1840s Grade 2 listed building, four bedrooms, original features, stable, *£25,000!*' I'd take the paper from her, point at the address: 'Look at *this*,' I'd say. 'So what's wrong with X street?' she'd ask. To which the answer would always be, too Catholic, too Protestant for you or for me. To which Ali eventually and reasonably enough asked, so what about this peace process we're supposed to be having?

Oh, yes, *that*.

So we went looking.

Here's a tip. If you are house-hunting in Belfast, make sure you do it in summer. That way you won't be surprised on I July, opening the blinds of the house you bought back in March, to find the street bedecked with bunting and loyalist flags; or by the sudden appearance on 9 August (the anniversary of internment) of republican emblems.

Ali and I spent the early summer of 1995 touring the city looking for a place where we could fit at a price we could afford. What was surprising, even to me, a native, was how many such places there seemed to be. Belfast, you have to understand, is a small city, population just over a third of a million. Everywhere is close to somewhere hairy. By the same token, every hairy is close to somewhere safer. Friends had assured us that the Ravenhill Road, parallel to the Ormeau Road, was OK. A few hundred yards to the left off the Ravenhill brought us on to the Cregagh Road. Approached by such side steps, the Cregagh Road was revealed to abound in affordable housing and to have the sort of urban village atmosphere familiar to me from places like Rusholme and Fallowfield in Manchester. Approached from the city centre, as I had always till then approached it, the Cregagh was heralded by a giant mural of UVF gunmen.

It was one of the victories of the paramilitaries – in fact probably their only undisputed victory – that they managed to impose, through flags and murals and painted kerbstones, their imprint on entire districts, obliterating all such quirks. After several visits to a house off the Cregagh Road, Ali and I decided to trust our instincts rather than the murals. It was in every sense the best move we ever made – though there was a moment in our first summer there, the summer of the first Drumcree stand-off, when we might have thought otherwise. Loyalist protestors had threatened to bring the whole of Northern Ireland to a halt. In the city centre, shops shut early, and bars and restaurants were soon persuaded to follow suit. On the Cregagh Road little moved after 6 p.m. Ali and I felt remote from our friends elsewhere in the city. We played a lot of Scrabble. I was, on occasion, driven to the extreme measure of working in the evening.

Six and a bit years later when we came to move again, our house had nearly trebled in price, in part a result of Belfast belatedly being caught by the housing boom, in part a result of boundaries being redrawn – the boundaries of the possible – by people doing exactly what we had done, taking a small step to the side, on all sides.

With the money we made we could have moved pretty much wherever we wanted to in the city. We stayed in the east. You still got more house for your money on this side of town, but also – how do I put this? – after six and a bit years we liked the look of the city from here. It's a much-abused term in Northern Ireland, but I think what we felt was a sense of community.

While we were on the Cregagh Road, another friend's father died. The funeral service was in a church down the road towards the centre of town, an all too imaginable stone's throw from the enormous UVF mural. I had passed the church scores of times without registering it was Catholic. My friend said that even in the worst years his father had refused to move because he didn't want the parish to die. It struck me as an impulse more civic than religious. The city could not bear too much division. Too much one religion or another.

I am always astounded when I hear it said that not letting the conflict affect how you live is an apolitical stance.

Belfast is still a divided city. Only recently a young, mixed couple of our acquaintance were 'advised' by someone where they lived in north Belfast that they might be best seeking alternative accommodation. (They have moved east, close to us.) Belfast is also, increasingly, a city of downtown apartments. Many of these developments are in parts of the city centre bombed half to death in the Seventies. Here 'mixed' means privately owned and housing association administered, high-spec and low-rent. Religious mixture is either a given or an irrelevance. With a few notable exceptions, they are architecturally uninspiring, to say the least. But I love every square, unaligned foot of them.

Too plain never killed anybody.

Daily Telegraph, June 2003

Accommodation and apartmentality

Towards the end of 1987 I started work on my second novel. The first had been set in Belfast in the summer of 1969. This one was to be set in the city's (then) here and now. The snag was I was living in Manchester. A few years before this would scarcely have mattered. For most of the Seventies and early Eighties change in Belfast had largely been a question of subtraction. CEB Brett's seminal *Buildings of Belfast*, first published in 1967, had been reissued in 1985 with footnotes detailing the fate of this 'very individual' city's buildings of note: 'bombed...demolished...demolished for purely economic reasons...bombed, burnt out and demolished.' By the time I started my novel, however, the IRA's car bombing campaign had been scaled down – or simply stymied by the city's security measures, which had themselves turned the centre into a dead zone after dark – and much of the wholesale housing clearance associated with the building of the new urban motorway, the Westlink, was complete.

On my recent visits home I had discovered that construction was beginning to outstrip destruction. So much so, in fact, that I was repeatedly having to revise the city I was writing for my characters to live in. I took to coming back for longer, walking whenever possible, as a friend in Manchester had advised I do on moving there to see how the city connects. I also took to carrying a camera. I had no illusions about the artistic merit of my photographs. The camera was simply a box for transporting memories back to my desk. I photographed the fence behind which the foundations were being dug for the Castlecourt shopping centre; I photographed the half-clad skeleton of Tollgate House, among the city centre's first apartment developments, at the corner of Sandy Row and Bradbury Place. (Yuppie flats, people muttered darkly, though in fact the Student Housing Association was involved in their building.) I was particularly pleased to carry away in my box an image of a restaurant that had recently opened on the first floor of the just-built Lesley House in Shaftesbury Square, Scruples Chicken Ranch.

Scruples was a surprisingly (or perhaps not so surprisingly) popular word in the unscrupulous Eighties. The decade had been heralded by the Judith Krantz novel of that name and, in a market made hungry by Trivial Pursuit, there was even a Scruples board game. For a while I toyed with the idea of putting one of my characters to work – unhappily – in the Chicken Ranch. 'You've read the book,' he would say, 'you've played the game, now eat the shit!' In the end I made him assistant manager of a bookstore chain (modelled on Waterstone's) which prided itself on blending in so well with its adopted cities that everyone, everywhere, imagined they were local.

Still, the point remained. Change, far from being a barrier to writing the novel, was going to be one of its central themes.

I was encouraged in this by another book, Jonathan Bardon's *Belfast, an Illustrated History,* surely a contender for the title of most important book published here in the last quarter of a century: a 300-page reminder that Belfast was not – as it so often appeared – static, stalemated, but was, like all cities, perpetually in process. It's hard to overstate the liberating effect of this thought on an imagination shaped in large part by the polarities of the Seventies.

Ciaran Carson's *Belfast Confetti,* published in 1989, included an acknowledgement to Bardon's book, or at least to its bibliography. (I was working my way through the bibliography myself, having abandoned the memory box and moved back permanently to write the novel, now called *Fat Lad.*) Time and again in *Belfast Confetti* it is the mutability of the city, its resistance to definition, that Ciaran Carson writes about. In 'Revised Version' (a typical *Belfast Confetti* title) he refers to a photo from 1879 showing the clearance of Hercules Place to create Royal Avenue, on which was built the Grand Central Hotel, itself cleared to build Castlecourt...

Viewed in this way over many centuries, each version of the city is as temporary as a face pulled in the mirror.

Sixteen years on from the start of *Fat Lad,* the expression that novel was trying to catch has changed again, though perhaps something of the mood behind it remains the same. Scruples is gone. Lesley House is now home to Paul Rankin's Cayenne, which in turn is a revised version of his original

Roscoff's. You no longer hear talk of yuppie flats. Too many of them. Of us. Of you.

In some respects, most notably the reclamation and renovation of docklands and inner-city riversides, Belfast has mimicked changes in cities across the globe. In *Fat Lad* the Waterfront Hall is still a rumour, is still, in fact, a derelict cattle market. In the novel I have just finished, *That Which Was*, set in the year 2000, the Waterfront is already old hat: the Odyssey Arena, downriver, is the new attraction. Or newish. In the time it took me to write the novel, the Odyssey's ice hockey team, the Belfast Giants, had appeared, like Flann O'Brien's Furriskey, fully formed, become champions of Britain and very nearly disappeared again.

In other respects, Belfast has not followed trends but anticipated them. In his most celebrated book, *City of Quartz*, the Californian urban theorist Mike Davis writes of a 'fortress LA', characterised by paranoia over security, and 'architecturally policed' social boundaries. It is a city where public space represents threat, where those who can afford it withdraw whenever possible into their gated communities, and where surveillance is an ever-present obsession. Nothing unrecognisable in this to citizens of Belfast, who already by the time *City of Quartz* was published had experienced two decades of helicopter searchlights and ever more and ever higher walls between neighbouring – but no longer neighbourly – areas. (Admittedly we had to wait until a couple of years after Davis's book, until the year of ceasefires itself, to get the ultimate manifestation of our fear of public places: the wall dividing Alexandra Park.) But while the garish marking out of territory has long been the object of scorn and despair, it is apparent, wherever you look in Belfast today, that measures intended to thwart terrorism and sectarian confrontation have gradually merged with the instincts of the new 'apartmentalised' city.

When the main entrance to the Taughmonagh estate (erstwhile 'Tintown'), close to where I grew up, was bricked in some years back to allow for the building of apartments and townhouses, locals instantly dubbed the new divide the Berlin Wall. Such walls are now as common as peace lines. Elsewhere the exterior of a new apartment development at the junction of Sandy Row and Donegall Road (and dwarfing the Tollgate House flats) resembles nothing so much as a sheer cliff face. When the Rangers Supporters' Club opposite burned down, there was a suggestion – this being Belfast, Paranoia Central – that it was part of a plot to drive out the old working-class loyalist community. What is undeniable is that the landmark Sandy Row bonfire has been progressively squeezed. For many years it was on the site of the cliff-face flats, then, when that site was lost, on waste ground at the corner of Hope Street. (Waste ground...bonfire...*Hope* Street... You can see why setting fiction in Belfast at times can appear like an easy dot-to-dot.) Now that site too has gone, or at least has been hidden from the general view.

Of course there will be many for whom this is one of the unexpected blessings of the city's current makeover, but it is sobering to reflect, seeing the wooden-pallet towers vying with apartment blocks and American kit-hotels – like boys standing precariously on one another's shoulders to get their mugs in shot – that there is not in the whole of Belfast a single building that has endured for as long as the bonfire tradition.

Indeed, at this time of more than usually accelerated transition, much of new-build Belfast still has the air of theatrical flats and set dressing. There is a persistent rumour that the Odyssey's roof is only good for fifteen years. Fifteen or a hundred and fifty, however, the arena is a future generation's nostalgia. (Future generation, tell us, are you still building the big fires?) One of the best antidotes to despondency I know is a passage from the great Lewis Mumford's *The City in History* comparing cities to trees: 'once established,' Mumford writes, 'they must be destroyed to the roots before they cease to live: otherwise, even when the main stem is cut down, shoots will form about the base.'

This passage came back to me with renewed force as I looked at John Duncan's new exhibition of Belfast photographs, *Trees from Germany*, which begins with a mature tree being delivered to Waring Street by articulated lorry and ends with a view from the city's western fringe of six new houses. For all the varieties of damage that have been inflicted on it, for all the battles still to be fought over planning and conservation, Belfast, like any city worth its salt, is endlessly adaptable and, in every sense of the word, accommodating.

Trees from Germany, September 2003

Muggins

There is a piece of graffiti close to where I live in east Belfast. 'Muggins in this area is totally unexceptable. Anyone caught will be severly dealt with,' the adverb spelled in such a way as to simultaneously suggest possible amputation and beatings by the bunch.

In fact, this graffiti appears not once, but twice within a two-hundred-yard stretch of road: word for word, misspelling for misspelling, suggesting that the graffiti artist may have been working from a prepared text. If the texts prepared for the decommissioning body are as poorly drafted, it's maybe no wonder that it has taken us more than a decade to sort out the arms issue. 'I'm sorry, what does this say: take the *what* out of Irish *what?*'

It is of course a favourite Northern Irish pastime, laughing at the illiteracy of the paramilitaries. A class thing, some might say, but that would ignore the fact that those who laugh are as likely to come from within the community that the paramilitaries claim to represent. I prefer to think it is the justified scorn of people who know that all too often the yoke is on them. 'You can push us around now, but wait till we get you in the spelling-bee, then you're whupped.'

Now, however, the wall-writers have an unlikely ally in the person of Colombian Nobel laureate Gabriel Garcia Marquez, who this week was barred from a prestigious conference on the Spanish language after calling at a previous conference for the abolition of what he referred to as 'the terror of spelling'.

As someone who has spent more hours than he cares to remember trying to decipher other people's idiosyncratic word constructions, I have to say spelling has never seemed to me a terror, but rather a common courtesy. On the other hand, as the father of a three-year-old just beginning to ask questions about the words she speaks, I have to say that I am not entirely out of sympathy with Marquez. Any parent will tell you that there is no defeat greater than the phrase 'because it just is', but it is a phrase I find I am using more and more these days, as when playing I-spy at seven o'clock and trying to explain why something that begins with c can be either ceiling or curtain.

I only have the press headlines to go by, i.e. very little in the way of direct quotation, but I am guessing that Marquez's quarrel is with *standardised* spelling, which only became enforced with the invention of printing, that is, not much more than five hundred years ago. In those days, however, before the rise of Empire, both English and Spanish were strictly *regional* languages. I can't speak for Spanish, but today English is proliferating at such a rate, in such a variety of contexts, across such a range of continents and media, that the centuries-old spelling rules are left looking understandably arthritic.

There have always been writers of fiction who have attempted to spell words the way their characters actually pronounce them. But this phonetic spelling can be the most problematic. There is a world of difference between *outta* and *oughta*. With standardised spelling we at least know the word the character is saying. If the writer is skilled enough in other ways we will have no trouble hearing *how* the character says it. Though then again, I studied creative writing with Angela Carter, one of the most innovative English writers of the Sixties and Seventies, who cheerfully admitted she couldn't spell for carp. And what else is a copy editor for?

Which brings us back to the walls of east Belfast and the unexceptable muggins. When meaning is this unambiguous, what does it matter that the *g* is elided or that *exc* is doing the job of *acc*? I don't want to see the *g* back in muggings. I want to see an end to muggings, yes, but just as keenly an end to the paramilitaries' way of severly dealing with offenders, actual or alleged.

By the way, my spell-check pulled me up at least three times while I was writing this. Only one *t* in pastime, two *ms* – I knew it, honest, I knew it – in decommissioning, drafted with an *ft*. It is almost impossible with computers to spell badly, even if you want to, but good – that is accurate, standardised – spelling on its own does not make for writing, or walls, worth respecting.

Radio Ulster, September 2004

Murals

In the summer of 1980 a sixteen-year-old boy was shot dead by police in Belfast. The RUC constable who was later acquitted of murdering Michael McCartan claimed that he believed the teenager had pointed a gun at him. In fact, McCartan was carrying nothing more lethal than a paint brush with which he had just finished painting the word 'Provos' on the side of a house close to the Ormeau Bridge. For many people here, whatever their political views, the killing was – and remains – a shocking symbol of free expression forcibly silenced. It was a reminder too that in Belfast even the walls are significant.

In the decade that followed, a curious war-within-a-war was fought on the walls of republican areas of the city. Political murals – paintings executed on the gable-ends of buildings – appeared at an unprecedented rate. The artists, often teenagers with no formal training and with only the bare minimum of resources, were regularly harassed by police and soldiers. The murals themselves were vandalised by paint-bombs hurled from army Land Rovers.

Then, in the autumn of 1994, in the aftermath of the IRA ceasefire, there was a new and sustained outbreak of graffiti. As so often happens, here and elsewhere, the graffiti was painted over almost as soon as it appeared. What was unusual in this case, though, was that those doing the whitewashing came not from the city council but from Sinn Féin. The IRA's 'complete cessation of violence' had not included an end to so-called punishment attacks (baseball-bat beatings to you and me) on people the paramilitaries considered 'anti-social'. In fact, these had increased. The offending graffiti consisted of a variation on a simple theme: *Stop the beatings*. Its authors – opponents of the attacks, in some cases relatives of the victims – were concentrating their efforts on walls bearing Sinn Féin-sponsored murals.

The conclusion to be drawn was obvious. The murals of Belfast, once considered statements of radical opposition, had become institutionalised, an accepted, almost official part of city life; sabotaging them, rather than painting them, was the Nineties' danger sport.

Further evidence of the murals' new-found respectability came in June of this year when three were featured in a series of postcards published by the Ulster Card Company. The cards quickly became best-sellers. They were sold out yet again in the Northern Ireland Tourist Board shop when I went in recently hoping to buy a set. It was a cold November morning; it was hard to imagine anyone who wasn't born here wanting to be in Belfast. It seemed though that there were indeed tourists around.

'Those cards walk off the racks as soon as we put them out,' the shop assistant told me.

The mural series was the brainchild of Paul Lavery, a former marketing director at the Tourist Board. The Ulster Card Company, he says, was born out of a sense of frustration: until its arrival on the scene, the vast majority of 'Northern Irish' postcards were in fact produced in the Republic of Ireland and England. The picture, or pictures, they gave were far from adequate.

Belfast, Lavery points out, is no London or Dublin. It's a provincial city short on attractions. So, you have to ask yourself, what is there about it that's different? Twenty-five years of conflict, that's what.

Paul Lavery is the least cynical person you could hope to talk to. He has simply recognised the obvious fact that among the influx of tourists to Northern Ireland after the ceasefires were a significant number who wanted to see the place where the Troubles had happened. One of the most successful outlets for his cards is the Youth Hostel in Belfast's Donegall Road. Backpackers whose late Eighties' counterparts would have gone to Berlin or Prague are now including Belfast on their itineraries. Murals are not only what this new breed of tourists want, they are what they expect. Let's face it, they haven't come here for the weather.

Of course, any Belfast person who has ever had someone visit them from across the water or south of the border could have told you this. We have all acted as unofficial tour guides at one time or another, giving guests our own, inevitably partial versions of the city. (For visitors unlucky enough not to have a friend with a car, there were always the taxis which would show you the war-torn sights at a charge of anything up to £25 an hour.) For many years, official tours of the city scrupulously avoided all mention of the conflict. The cease-fires changed that as they changed so much else. Perhaps feeling that the story was over and therefore capable of being dispassionately assessed (i.e. packaged), Citybus began a new service offering what the ads promised was a 'better view' of the city and its recent troubled history. I was asked to report on one of the first excursions for a radio arts programme. I was struck by two things: how thorough and informative the tour actually was, and how uninterested the majority of the passengers were for large parts of the journey. They sat, cameras at the ready, waiting for something – *anything* – to snap. And they sat and they sat. And then a garishly painted wall hove into view on our left and the bus nearly cowped over with the sudden stampede.

In a conflict where the battle-zones were more often than not streets of ordinary-looking shops and houses, the murals are a godsend to tourists and tour operators alike.

The first recorded murals in Belfast date from around the turn of the century. To begin with they were a largely Protestant sport, painted to coincide with the annual twelfth of July parades and resembling nothing so much as petrified versions of the banners carried by the Orange lodges. Like the banners, nearly all these early examples featured King Billy crossing the river Boyne on a white horse.

The modern Belfast mural, however, in the form that it has become familiar around the world, did not begin in earnest until 1981, the year of the Hunger Strike when ten IRA and INLA prisoners starved themselves to death in the Maze prison. Out of the street protests in support of the hunger strikers, a new tradition of republican murals was born. Loyalists responded by revamping their own gable-ends, and before long no self-respecting working-class area was complete without at least one mural. (Note: *working-class*, don't bother going mural-hunting up the Malone Road.) They are in a sense adverts – billboard sites have been used as canvases on occasion – and not surprisingly this has made them as fascinating to sociologists as it has to tourists. (The acknowledged authority is Bill Rolston, senior lecturer in sociology at the University of Ulster, who has published several books on the subject.) If you want to understand Catholics and Protestants, the theory runs, take a look at what they paint on their walls.

The popular image is that, King Billy aside, there have only ever been two sorts of loyalist mural: threatening and more threatening. And it is true that down the years loyalist muralists have specialised, to the point of fixation, in masked men with guns, grouped around the insignia of the various Protestant terror groups: the UVF, the UDA, the UFF and, occasionally, the PAF and the RHC. There is much painting of flags. History is reduced to two or three dates: 1690 (the Battle of the Boyne), 1912 (the formation of the first Ulster Volunteer Force in opposition to Home Rule), and 1916 (the battle of the Somme, when thousands of the Ulster Volunteers died fighting for the British government they had been prepared fight against). There is a notably high incidence of black moustaches.

The peace process brought little in the way of fresh imagery or ideas. Indeed, the hooded gunmen seemed to become even more numerous. This has been taken to indicate the bankruptcy of the loyalist ideology: backward looking and innately militaristic, it cannot project a vision of the future. It has become almost standard when talking about 'Protestant identity' in Northern Ireland to preface it with the word 'crisis'. The extent of their confusion is often illustrated by reference to another mural, at 'Freedom Corner' on the Newtownards Road, in which the figure of Cuchulainn, the mythical Irish hero, is twinned with a uniformed UDA man under the heading 'Ulster's Past and Present Defenders'.

Republicans too have depicted their fair share of armed and masked men in their time; they too have their flags and their reduced view of history. Here again, 1916 is a big year, though not now for the Somme, of course, but the Easter Rising. The leaders of this rebellion, Connolly and Pearse, are popular subjects, though their appearances are far outnumbered by the 1981 hunger strikers, in particular Bobby Sands. Martyrs, as everyone knows, play a key role in republican mythology. It is for this reason that *they* invoke Cuchulainn: the symbol of the one who gave his life standing defiant against the many.

What has traditionally distinguished republican from loyalist murals, though, is their willingness to look outside Northern Ireland for inspiration. According to Bill Rolston, this is in part due to the ability of republicans as revolutionaries to make common cause with other revolutions, whereas the loyalists, defending the status quo, can do nothing but rehash the same old images. Over the years, therefore, the IRA has been portrayed in common cause with the ANC, the Sandinistas and, most frequently, the PLO.

(It's been a few years since the Palestinian connection was last made, but perhaps it's time it was revived, now that Amnesty International has highlighted the torture of Palestinian prisoners by Yasser Arafat's Palestinian police force: *IRA and PLO — Stop the beatings!*)

Much, too, has been made of the inclusion of images of
women in republican murals – something for which there is
no loyalist equivalent. Ireland has, of course, long been per-
sonified as a woman (Caithlin Ni Houlihan come on
down), but this image too has undergone a transformation
in recent times. Rolston comments favourably on one mural
which showed her not as a powerless victim, but as a 'young,
strong, blonde' woman.

Excuse me – young, strong, *blonde*: does that ring any
bells?

Admittedly that particular mural has long since been
painted over, replaced by a map of Ireland, overlaid with a
manacled hand clutching an Easter Lily (available on post-
card in most good newsagents): a reminder that the message
from the walls is constantly being revised.

With this in mind, I took a drive around the city a
couple of weeks back to see what was currently on offer.

With a very few exceptions, loyalist areas are still dominated by flags and crests and hoods and guns: 'Prepared for
peace, ready for war' is the slogan. There are still a dispro-
portionate number of black moustaches. There are, too,
murals calling for the release of 'POWs', though nothing
like on the scale of the republican side, where the green
ribbon of the *Saoirse* campaign now regularly replaces the X
beneath 'Vote Sinn Féin'. For the rest, the autumn '96
murals here are a curious mix of old and new. On the
Whiterock Road a half-finished gable-end looks like a wall-
sized painting by numbers; off Shaws Road a mural saying
'No Return to Stormont' is badly in need of repair. There
are numerous images of British soldiers in retreat ('Slan'
read the subtitles: 'Slan abhaile') and at every turn signs pro-
claim 'RUC Out'. Some of these clearly belong to the

period immediately following the ceasefire, but elsewhere murals from that time have already been submerged beneath newer paintings. Among the most recent are murals commemorating last year's 150th anniversary of the Famine, though one Falls Road wall states categorically 'There was no Famine'. This theme of British blame is taken up again on the Springfield Road, where a Famine family are portrayed as victims of 'the Irish Holocaust', while another mural combines Famine imagery with a memorial to the 1981 hunger strikers. Bobby Sands, the first hunger striker to die, still looks down from several walls, in Laburnum Way, where he once lived, and in Sevastopol Street, on the side of the Sinn Féin Headquarters. What images there are of the IRA are evidently old, so that it's easy to forget that not only have they not gone away, but they have detonated a couple of tons of explosives in the last nine months.

I drove round and round, up the Shankill, down the Falls, across the Lagan to east Belfast, back across to the north, through the city centre to the south, and then I did it all again. I lost count of the number of walls I had stared at, and as the details began to run together all I was left with was an overriding impression of kitsch.

No, it wasn't just those black moustaches; it wasn't the uniformed loyalists, crouching and stretching in perfect symmetry like some grotesque parody of a boy band; it wasn't even that the whole gaudy succession, loyalist and republican, resembled the tea-towel rack in a crap seaside souvenir shop. This was kitsch of an altogether higher order.

In *The Unbearable Lightness of Being* Milan Kundera defines kitsch as, essentially, that which denies the existence of shit, since kitsch excludes 'everything from its purview which is unacceptable in human existence', or even, as he goes on to say, unacceptable to a particular ideology: 'whenever a single political movement corners power we find ourselves in the realm of *totalitarian* kitsch.'

If the Belfast murals are indeed adverts then they are as much for the benefit of the local inhabitants as they are for tourists. They are a reminder of who has cornered power in this district or that. (It is inconceivable that a UDA mural would appear in a UVF-dominated area, or an INLA one in an IRA stronghold.) This is why critical voices, and graffiti, are so unacceptable.

And despite their guns and their menace, there is precious little shit here, the real shit truth of our quarter-century war, I mean: a war for the most part of bombs in cars and bullets in the back of the head, a war in which the IRA killed more Irish citizens than English soldiers, in which the UVF and UFF killed many times more Catholic civilians than republican combatants.

Oddly, or perhaps I should say fittingly, the one glimpse of veracity I saw on my last tour was also one of the nastiest. On a wall off the Shankill Road, a UVF man takes a sledgehammer to a front door, while two colleagues stand by, machine guns at the ready. Yes, I thought, that's what it was like: fucking foul murder.

I confess to disappointment that not once did I see *Stop the beatings* graffiti. Maybe after four hundred attacks and more and no let-up in sight, the protesters have lost heart. A pity (though let's face it, I didn't get out of the car with my spray can), in their absence there is little to remind tourists that the murals they so happily snap hide some very bad shit indeed.

In Dublin, autumn 1996

Kerbstones

In August 1969, eight years almost to the day after the advent of the Berlin Wall, rioting in Belfast led to the hasty erection of a peace-line between the Protestant Shankill and Catholic Falls Road, or rather, for most of its length, between the Shankill and Springfield Roads. Thirty-five years on – fifteen years from the fall of the Berlin wall, ten years from the IRA ceasefire, six years on from the Good Friday Agreement – that 'temporary' peace-line, reinforced and extended to over half a mile, still stands, as do the couple of dozen others created in its image in various contentious parts of the city. The greatest concentration, like the greatest concentration of murders during the conflict, is in north Belfast, including one, erected since the Agreement, through the middle of a public park.

Protestants and Catholics may, for the most part, have stopped killing one another, but that is not to say that they are ready to live side by side.

This was never, by any stretch of the imagination, an integrated city, but it is a more profoundly divided one now than at any time in its history. Whereas two-thirds of Belfast citizens were estimated to be living in segregated streets in the 1960s, by the 1980s the figure had risen to four-fifths. Evidence suggests that figure has gone on rising. In his book *The Trouble With Guns*, writer and magazine editor Malachi O'Doherty, a Catholic by birth, tells how during the riots of 1969 he was trying to make his way home from the Shankill Road where he was then working as a barman. Finding himself lost he asked for — and was given — directions to the Falls. It is almost impossible to imagine such a scenario today. Nor is it easy to see how the current divisions can be reversed. Where once there were through-roads now there are cul-de-sacs; housing at many traditional flashpoints has been cleared altogether and retail developments, industrial parks, even motorways built as de facto buffer zones. A wall, in time, can be dismantled, but how in the world do you overcome six lanes of traffic?

With their backs turned to one another, these segregated areas are often further divided into paramilitary zones of influence. If flags and painted kerbstones — green white and orange or red white and blue — will tell you whether you are in a Catholic or Protestant part of town, murals are usually the best guide to which organisation holds sway there. A BBC Northern Ireland investigation earlier this month into antagonisms between loyalist paramilitaries was aptly entitled 'Feudal Times'. Though east Belfast has been the focus of the most recent feud, the bloodiest and most protracted remains that which in the summer of 2000 split the Shankill Road, Korea-like, between an upper (UVF) end and a lower (UDA) one. Scores of families were put out of their homes. According to one contributor to 'Feudal Times', the Road is still traumatised by the events.

My mother's family are Shankill people. A few years back my brother and I drove an uncle, home from Australia, around the streets where he had grown up. He was visibly shaken by the depredations.

It is all the more remarkable, then, that the Shankill has just picked up a 'Keep Britain Tidy Award' after an initiative that has seen the removal of twenty-seven murals, sectarian graffiti and paint from seven thousand metres of kerb-stones. This is not – as one over-enthusiastic press agency suggested – 'the last vestiges of the Troubles [being] scrubbed away', but it is a start.

In another recent development, senior figures in Sinn Féin and the Democratic Unionist Party issued what appear to have been synchronised calls for a quiet summer in Belfast. (Summers here have traditionally been hot for all the wrong reasons.) Mobile phones, meanwhile, have been issued to community workers either side of certain of the peace-lines to allow them to communicate and mediate at the first signs of trouble.

And all the time housing is returning to the city centre itself, reversing decades of population decline. In keeping with other cities in Britain and Ireland, much of this housing consists of apartments for young singles: 'yuppie flats' as they are still somewhat anachronistically referred to. So far these developments have been largely free of sectarian tension and iconography, though only last month there were ugly demonstrations outside an apartment block on Sandy Row, a working-class Protestant district behind the city's 'golden mile' of restaurants and bars, after rumours that an Irish flag had been waved from one of the windows. Of even greater concern are the attacks in both Catholic and Protestant parts of the city on members of Belfast's still small ethnic communities. In loyalist areas in particular there has been clear evidence of paramilitary involvement.

It seems that while the peace-lines are undeniably popular with those living within a stone's — or a petrol bomb's — throw of the other side (and who knows, were I living there myself they might be popular with me), they have perpetuated into our heavily processed peace a world-view where there are really only two types of people: 'us' and 'not-us'.

There are still many thousands of metres of kerbstones to go.

Index on Censorship, June 2004

Open up

On the last Saturday of June 1966, four young barmen coming off work at Belfast's International Hotel went in search of a late-night drink. They found it in the Malvern Arms off the Shankill Road. In the early hours of the following morning, one of the four, Peter Ward, was shot and killed as he left the bar by the side door. Two of his companions were critically wounded. The International barmen were all Catholics; the Shankill Road, as most people know, is a bastion of working-class Protestantism. It is easy at this remove to wonder why on earth Peter Ward and his friends should have chosen the Malvern Arms to drink in. The remarkable thing about that time, however, was that their going there was entirely *un*remarkable. (At least one of the four was on first name terms with the bar owner.) On the other side, my own father, a Protestant, was still drinking in bars on the Falls as late as spring 1971.

All of which might lead you reasonably to conclude that, rather than the violence of the last thirty years being the inevitable consequence of a divided city, Belfast is the profoundly divided city it is today because of the violence.

Of course, there have always been areas here which are predominantly (even exclusively) Protestant or Catholic – a situation greatly exacerbated by the massive population influx that accompanied the city's rapid industrialisation in the nineteenth century. Immigrants from the country tended to cluster around their respective churches. (This explains why most of the famous working-class Protestant areas are Church of Ireland and not Presbyterian, as popularly supposed.) A city once noted for its religious tolerance quickly became a by-word for bigotry and mayhem.

Through all the riots that flared periodically into our own century, however, the primary lines of communication, that is, the streets themselves, remained open. The unique legacy of our own era's Troubles is that many of those lines are now not only closed, but permanently severed.

More depressing than any of Belfast's crude peace-lines is the subtle segregation of the newer housing developments, with built-in buffer zones between them and other, religiously opposed developments.

I recently drove around the Woodvale Road, where my mother's family come from. Some of my earliest memories are of walking from the Woodvale across the Crumlin Road and through Ardoyne to visit relatives on the Oldpark, but driving around the side streets I was soon lost in a one-way system that seemed to throw up a bigger, more militaristic mural at every turn. I had spent a significant portion of my childhood around here, but now I was disoriented and not a little scared. I have never seen so many cul-de-sacs.

Nor is this turning inwards merely architectural. More and more imagination seems to be expended on drawing ever finer distinctions between the city's constituent parts. Many Belfast people, for instance, will tell you that they have no recollection of a district known as 'the Lower Ormeau'. If anything, this obsession has become more pronounced since the beginning of our long and torturous peace process. Laudable aims like self-empowerment and self-confidence appear at times to have been pursued without much in the way of self-scrutiny or self-criticism. All too often our minutely defined communities can present to their nearest neighbours at best a smug, at worst a hostile face.

A city is, or ought to be, a place of mixture and exchange. Confronted with the kind of calculated division just described, the very least a city needs is an open, permissive centre into which citizens can, if they wish, escape, night as well as day. Infamously, by the mid-1970s Belfast's non-sectarian city centre had shrunk to an inner ring, a few hundred yards in diameter, surrounded by gates which were locked at 9 p.m. Many of the victims of the murder gangs were literally picked off as they walked around the circumference.

If the centre is the city's heart, Belfast's back then was barely beating.

Then again, if there is one thing greater than a city's resilience, it is its sheer longevity. What can, measured against the average human life-span, feel like long years of near death, may prove in the longer term to be nothing more serious than the city holding its breath.

The day before yesterday, I had to point out to a writer friend – at thirty, only eight years my junior – where exactly the security gates had been.

In the centre at any rate, Belfast has been tackling the reality and the image of its darker days for the best part of twenty years. Most importantly, it has expanded the perimeter of the neutral centre. Indeed, one of our newest bars, aptly named (though not for its decor or ambience) the Edge, takes that centre to its easternmost limit, with a deck practically overhanging the river Lagan, on the far bank of which the Sirocco Works, once one of the giants of Belfast industry, awaits its own leisure makeover.

Love it or loathe it (myself, I'm undecided: put me, for the minute, in the *loave* camp), the Laganside development, of which the Edge is a part, has changed the character of Belfast city centre, and no element more so than the Waterfront concert hall, which now dramatically closes the vista as you look past the Royal Courts of Justice from the City Hall. Though it has not yet – and may never – become the 'People's Palace' its champions had hoped it would, the Waterfront has provided a new cultural focus, if not through its programme, then at the very least through the events which take place in the pedestrianised precinct that surrounds it.

High on my list of things I thought I'd never live to see has got to be this summer's open-air gig there by Dogstar. That's Dogstar as in Keanu-Reeves-on-bass Dogstar. It's fashionable, I know, to knock Keanu's rock 'n' roll ambitions (fashionable, and I have to say, having stood through the hour-long Dogstar set, justifiable), but some part of me thought all of us in the audience had come a long way, metaphorically speaking, to be standing in a car park on the site of the old Oxford Street bus station, watching one of the Nineties' biggest movie stars.

Well you didn't think anyone was looking at the rest of the band, did you?

In fact, though, the most exhilarating and visually stim-ulating part of that particular day for me had finished hours before Dogstar took the stage, when the Belfast Carnival stopped traffic for an hour on its passage through the centre of town. Now, higher even than Keanu in a car park on that list of things I thought I'd never see is hundreds of Northern Irish people, young and not-so, male and female, in feathers and face paint (and sometimes little more) dancing the salsa in Royal Avenue. Mind you, it strikes me as appropriate that, in a city where large numbers of people like nothing better than to process down the middle of the road, the one genuinely cross-community addition to the cultural calendar since the ceasefires should be a street parade; appropriate, too, that from its inception the carnival has sashayed its way to the Waterfront precinct, bypassing the more traditional, but politically loaded, rallying point in front of the City Hall.

Belfast lost more than the life of one of its citizens the night the International barmen were gunned down outside the Malvern Arms. Thirty-three years on, there is still much to recover. We may as well set our sights high. After all, in the words of the great urban historian Lewis Mumford, the city is the 'symbol of the possible. Utopia [is] part of its constitution'.

Or, in the words of John Lydon, Belfast: 'Open up'.

The Irish Times, October 1999

Stranger here myself

My friend Andy is in town. My friend Liz has rung to tell
me to ring her back when he's rung me. We have been com-
plicating arrangements like this for fifteen years. Then, I had
just returned from Manchester to write my second novel.
Andy was in a flat off the Lisburn Road making his fourth
album, *Out There*. He had a song on it called 'Waiting for the
39' after the bus down the Lisburn Road into town. Now
Andy is in Australia, back on tour twice a year.

He rings. 'Half nine,' I say, as I always do, and then,
thinking I'm saying something new, 'Bar Bacca.'

Bar Bacca is just behind our old meeting place, the
Crown Bar. Just behind and a million miles from. The theme
is Eastern — candles, cushions, sunken sofas, great big
Buddha — though the east it most recalls is Berlin's when I
first visited at the end of the Eighties. In fact, if Bar Bacca
has a drawback, that's it: when you walk out the door you're
not actually in Prenzlauer Berg.

At half nine plus five, Andy appears. 'They've changed the 39 to the 9A,' he says. It's the new Metrolink system, I tell him. More buses, less euphony. At half nine plus ten he says, 'So where will we go when Liz gets here?' It seems I wasn't saying anything new when I said Bar Bacca. It seems I have been saying Bar Bacca for the last five years and that for five years Liz has been saying that Bar Bacca is too loud for the catching-up chat we want to have.

'It's usually Ten Square after this,' Andy says, and I remember, just after the hotel opened at the back of the City Hall, a couple of nights when we were the only customers in its ground-floor bar. That was before *Cosmopolitan* voted Ten Square one of its six sexiest weekend retreats.

'It'll be packed,' I say.

'So what about all these new places?' Andy asks.

It's got to that even in Belfast. Five years is old.

Liz arrives. 'Help me,' I say the second after she says it's a bit loud, 'Andy wants to go somewhere really new.'

We have a drink to think.

'I know,' I say. 'Malmaison.'

Malmaison was recently named one of the world's Hot New Hotels by Condé Nast. Belfast is suddenly coming down with interesting hotel facts, at least more interesting than the Europa being the most bombed hotel in the world, though even in 1990 when the three of us started going out for drinks together that had grown a bit hoary. That was part of what the novel I was writing was about; part of the background to *Out There*.

Malmaison is just up the street from the enormous hole in the ground that will soon be the Victoria Centre, Belfast's largest retail development. It is the makeover of a previous hot new place to go, the McCausland, which was itself a renovation of a nineteenth-century seed warehouse. A pretty spectacular seed warehouse, it has to be said. Andy, Liz and I fetch up there a little after eleven. (Make that two drinks to think in Bar Bacca.) The door from the street into the bar is locked, but undeterred we breeze in by the lobby entrance. Lots of purples and reds, chairs that look like they were liberated from the churches we have deserted for Sainsbury's on a Sunday. The barman asks us are we residents. By coincidence – happy, we think – Andy is going to be a resident in a couple of nights' time, after his Belfast gig.

'But, not at the moment?' the barman says.

No, not at the moment.

'Then, I'm afraid...' the barman spreads his hands.

We are staggered. You have to understand, late-night drinking in Belfast has been an established fact for close on two decades: a long story, but a desire to draw support away from paramilitary drinking clubs is involved.

Maybe the lure of drinking clubs is as past-tense as the Europa's most-bombed gong. Maybe we just caught Malmaison on a bad night. The website invites you to come into the bar any day of the week between eleven in the morning and midnight. Mind you, the website also tells you that they have nicknamed the hotel 'Mal Bellefast' and promises guests 'more than a drop of the blarney'. That'll be Blarney as in County Cork. That'll be the cliché predating the 'Bad but Beautiful', which itself predates the one I may be peddling of Belfast the butterfly emerging from its chrysalis.

It's not the fact of change that is new in Belfast, it's the speed. I always fancied I knew the city pretty well, and not just as a writer. Even in the very worst times, Belfast never lacked tourists. What it lacked was a tourist infrastructure.

Like most people with a spare room (or floor) and a car, I have been a hotelier and a tour guide, though I confess I once drove the American novelist – and Van Morrison fan – Rick Moody around east Belfast for an hour failing to find Cyprus Avenue.

(You can come back now, Rick, I drive up it every day on my way home, and the music journalist Stuart Bailie does a tour of Van-related sites: Cyprus Avenue, Hyndford Street, Beechie river, Davey's chipper...)

The Malmaison's leap into the limelight took me by surprise. I didn't even know the McCausland had gone. I used to worry when I didn't recognise band names on bills posted outside bars. These days I don't even recognise the bars. Like the Potthouse. You would think you couldn't miss the Potthouse. In an area – the slow-to-the-tongue 'Cathedral Quarter' – where blending in with the old commercial architecture is the norm, it jumps out: three floors of solid glass all lit up in yellow. Yet the first I knew of it opening was reading a review of it in the *Observer*.

The Potthouse is the first place we see on stepping out the Malmaison's doors. This part of town, the streets around High Street and the landmark Albert Clock, is where Belfast began and is the new nightlife centre, a mile or so removed from the Shaftesbury Square/university area that was, all through my teens and twenties, the one place where you felt free of the baleful influence of the balaclava brigades. Shaftesbury Square and the university area are still teeming at the weekends. If you've seen documentaries about binge drinking in your part of the world, you've been there already.

So down to the Potthouse we go. There has been a fashion show earlier in the evening. Liz was on the catwalk.

The bar is full of fashion-show people. Very beautiful, very inclined to talk very loudly very close to one another's faces (and Liz's, those who know her). We leave again. It's now half eleven. The Metrolink, like Citybus which it replaced, has stopped running. But this is not a problem. Belfast always was a very walkable city. The problem was you most often felt like running. There is, even ten years after the ceasefires, and even with the paramilitaries' occasionally liberal interpretation of the term, something thrilling to someone of my age, bumping around these streets late on a summer's night. Temple Bar in Dublin is supposed to be the model, but Temple Bar is more like Shaftesbury Square these days.

This reminds me more of Canal Street when I lived in Manchester, before Canal Street became Temple Bar too. And we are not stuck for choice. A couple of hundred yards away there is the guaranteed welcome of the John Hewitt. Closer, but less predictably congenial, is the Northern Whig, named for the newspaper once published in the building, and displaying an ironic take on barroom politics in the shape of cast-off statues from Soviet-era Prague. But this is a night for somewhere we've never been before. Ali, my wife, just moved offices down this end of town. She has told me of another place. We cut back across High Street and up the narrow Church Lane and find it: Nicholl Bar Brasserie. I remember this under another name when it advertised itself as, at seven feet wide, the smallest bar in Belfast. (I tried to go in once, but someone else was already in it.) Nicholl isn't a whole lot wider. There are maybe ten customers downstairs when we arrive and it's pretty full. Ten customers and no two pairs of them appearing in the same film; a few of them aren't even in colour. Despite the 'brasserie', Nicholl at this time of the night is all bar, and none the worse for that. It's exactly what we've been looking for. It's what Belfast lost and may be finding again. When we leave, loose of limb, before the new chucking out time of one o'clock, it doesn't matter that it's not Prenzlauer Berg out there.

I mention this, a couple of Sundays later, to a German journalist who has flown in on one of the new direct flights from Berlin. I take her on a tour. We drive into town behind the 9A along the Lisburn Road. I tell her about the Northern Ireland Tourist Board initiative, 'Be a Tourist at Home'. I tell her I would have to start with the Lisburn Road. I once rented a house here, but in the decade since I decamped to east Belfast I have often felt like a stranger coming back. There has been no Condé Nast or *Cosmopolitan* poll, but I would defy anyone to show me a more chic mile and a half in Ireland.

We wind up in the Cathedral Quarter. I am talking up Belfast's radical heritage when I suddenly blurt, 'I love this city.' And standing on Donegall Street on a sunny Sunday morning, I am in no doubt I do. Whether despite or due to the attempts to market it, something distinctive really has taken root in this part of town in recent years.

But then... Directly across the street from us is the shuttered entrance to the North Street Arcade, which until it caught fire in May 2004 – at both ends simultaneously – was one of the finest examples of 1930s architecture in the city and home to some of Belfast's most individual businesses and organisations: the Cathedral Quarter Arts Festival; Factotum, publishers of the *Vacuum* free newspaper; the latest in a long line of record shops belonging to Terri

Hooley, who twenty-five years ago took the Undertones into a studio down an entry off Donegall Street to record 'Teenage Kicks'. Terri's hand might not have been too far from the aerosol that has written across the shutters, what many people believe, 'they burnt us out'.

There are rumours of a multi-storey car park in the vicinity; more-than rumours of a retail development to eclipse the Victoria Centre; fears that the Cathedral Quarter was all along a cover for the developers' long-term ambitions.

I hope these fears are unfounded. I hope that in pursuit of Urban Outfitters the developers don't make strangers of a whole lot more of Belfast's citizens.

Guardian, August 2005

The Hewitt

A couple of weeks ago I made a surprising discovery: there are now bars in Belfast city centre which I have not been in. Not because I am scared to go into them, or otherwise disinclined, but simply because there are too many of them to get round. In any other city of a comparable size, I realise, this would hardly be a startling claim. The bombing campaigns of the 1970s, however, meant that scarcely a week passed without another bar closing or being obliterated. I reckon Belfast came out of that most damaging decade of our Troubles with something under half the bars, clubs and hotels it went in with. The revival, until recent times, was slow and uneven. Well into the Eighties, I remember standing in the Crown Bar in a group of writers that included Martin Amis (sorry, on the edge of a group of writers that included Martin Amis), who had just finished a reading in a nearby arts centre. The conversation turned at one stage to the

Crown's magnificent stained glass windows, and how on earth they had survived the repeated bomb attacks on the Europa Hotel immediately across the road. Later that night, Robinson's bar, adjoining the Crown, and like the Crown dating from the turn of the century, was gutted by an incendiary device, planted perhaps at the very time when we were in the Crown talking about bomb-blasts past.

Robinson's was in time rebuilt and has again become one of Belfast's most popular bars, or rather bar *complexes*, ranging as it does over three floors. One recent addition to the city's nightlife indeed is its refurbished basement bar, named for the city centre's postcode, BT1. BT1 is relatively rare among the new generation of Belfast bars in the adventurousness of its design. (A few years back we had a spate of retro 'spirit grocers' and 'general merchants'. The theme here seemed to be a non-contentious past, when Guinness was good for you and a pound of sugar was a pound of sugar in anybody's language.) BT1 also features Belfast's first unisex toilets, a ploy perhaps to shame Belfast men into doing more than running a bit of cold water over three fingers of their right hand when they have finished peeing. I like BT1 a lot.

Not long after it opened I received an invitation to the opening of another bar, in Donegall Street, on the northern side of the city centre. Originally laid out at the turn of the eighteenth century, Donegall Street was badly mauled by the bombers. In March 1972 seven people died in an explosion outside the offices of the *News Letter*, one of two Belfast morning papers then based on the street. There were, furthermore, several sectarian murders in the surrounding streets. Some scars take longer to fade than others. For years, this part of town gave me the creeps.

Donegall Street, however, is also home to Belfast's Church of Ireland cathedral and is set to become the main thoroughfare in a proposed 'Cathedral Quarter', a mix of affordable apartments, artists' studios, cafés and shops, intended to emulate Dublin's Temple Bar. So, the arrival of any new bar on the street would be significant. It is arguable, though, that there will not, for a good many years, be a more important newcomer anywhere in the city than the bar which was officially opened on the last Saturday night in February.

Nor one with a more unlikely name. The John Hewitt is named for one of Belfast's most highly regarded poets, who died, aged seventy-nine, in 1987. According to Edna Longley, Professor of English at Queen's University Belfast, Hewitt's 'cross-sectarian ideal of Regionalism' was the well-spring for the upsurge in cultural activity in post-war Belfast and had a profound influence on the generation of poets that emerged in the 1960s, among them Edna Longley's own husband, Michael. Michael Longley, who along with four other of the city's leading poets read Hewitt's verse at the opening and who, with Hewitt's niece, unveiled a com-memorative plaque, remembered what it was like going out for a drink with Hewitt: the elderly poet would always order a half of Bass to Michael's pint, and if Michael were to suggest a second drink, would ask rather sternly if it wasn't time they were going.

Naming a bar after John Hewitt, joked Longley, was a little like naming a massage parlour after Mother Theresa.

In fact, despite talk of locating a Writers' Square close to the bar, Hewitt's reputation as a poet only partly explains the choice of the name. Just as important is that 'cross-sec-tarian ideal' Edna Longley refers to.

John Hewitt was a socialist, whose politics probably prevented him being appointed Director of the Ulster Museum, where he was for many years keeper of the fine art collection. Protestant by birth, he was a direct political descendent of the Belfast Presbyterians who at the end of the eighteenth century were the prime movers in the founding of the Society of United Irishmen. He represented a strand of radical humanism that was squeezed from both sides by the extremism which fuelled three decades of violence. Squeezed but never completely crushed.

Next door to the bar that bears his name is the Belfast Unemployed Resource Centre, opened by Hewitt on May Day 1985. It is the BURC which owns and manages the John Hewitt bar. To my knowledge, this is a unique venture for an organisation such as the BURC. The brainchild of the Resource Centre's Brendan Mackin, the bar has been six years in the planning. After overheads have been met, all profits from the John Hewitt will be directed towards projects to help the disadvantaged and unemployed.

This is reason enough to go there, but on the bar's opening night, Brendan Mackin spoke passionately about his desire to see created in the city centre an environment where people could go not to *avoid* talking politics, but to talk politics – art, whatever else they felt like – free from fear.

For the sad truth is that down the years, bars and clubs have repeatedly been targeted by terrorists. Often the mere choice of where you spend your nights out is taken as an indication of your religious or political beliefs. Only the week before the John Hewitt opened, two teenagers were picked up as they left a nightclub in the Co. Armagh town of Tandragee and were brutally murdered in an incident thought to have been connected to a loyalist feud. (A feud which, police insist, neither of the teenagers had any part in.) A society that cannot provide its citizens with opportunities to socialise in safety is unlikely to remain healthy for long.

On the last Saturday night in February, I was reminded how noble a thing is a *public* house. Fond as I am of BTI – beautiful and all as the Crown is – I think the John Hewitt could be the finest public house I have ever been in.

The Irish Times, April 2000

Linen Hall

I am a thirty-nine-year-old Northern Irish male who has only held a driving licence for the last four years. Which is to say that for roughly half my adult Northern Irish male life I carried no photographic identification. During this time I travelled a lot between Belfast and England and, like most relatively young, badly dressed Northern Irish males, I often found myself in airports chatting to Special Branch officers keen that I prove that I was who I said I was. On one occasion, clearly in desperation, I produced my membership card for the Linen Hall Library, or rather, as the card said in those days, for 'The Belfast Library and Society for Promoting Knowledge'.

The Special Branch officer read these words aloud and laughed. Oh, boy, did he laugh. 'Belfast,' he said. 'Promoting knowledge,' he said. 'That's a good one.'

This was, admittedly, at a time when a small but head-line grabbing minority of people here were still demon-strating, more or less daily, their knowledge of how to murder and mangle their fellow citizens. I could nearly see the Special Branch man's point. Nearly.

The truth is the Belfast Library and Society for Promoting Knowledge has, for two centuries, been the best advert for the fact that there is – thankfully – more to culture and politics in this part of Ireland than meets the eye.

The Library takes its more familiar name from its early home in what was then the commercial heart of the city, the White Linen Hall. There was also a Brown Linen Hall and a Linen Hall Street. Belfast in those late-eighteenth-century days was practically made of linen. Its merchants were inter-national in outlook, radical in politics (Belfast was the first city to send its congratulations to revolutionary France), and for the most part Presbyterian. Their political legacy was the Society of United Irishmen, who in 1798 led a doomed rebellion in the name of Catholic, Protestant and Dissenter, their cultural legacy the Linen Hall library. Thomas Russell, the Linen Hall's first librarian, was actually hanged for treason in 1803.

When the White Linen Hall was replaced by a grand, new City Hall early last century, the library moved across the street to – what else? – a converted linen warehouse. I first went there in the early Eighties. Marcus Patten's *Central Belfast Historical Gazetteer* captures the atmosphere then per-fectly. 'Up a steep stone staircase with polished brass central handrail, is a treasure trove of Irish history and literature, where unique records are scattered about with charming (and sometimes alarming) insouciance – at one stage several decades of the *Belfast Newsletter* were stored in the Gents.'

In recent decades the Linen Hall has been famed far beyond Northern Ireland for its unique political collection. There, in the library's attic – previously used for who knows what linen practices – could be found handbills from student demonstrations, transcripts from terrorist murder trials, loyalist and republican song books, mugs decorated with Ian Paisley's mug.... You name it – no matter how ephemeral – if it was Troubles-related, the political collection had it. The Linen Hall collected without partiality: Protestant, Catholic and Dissenter.

In January 1994 the Provisional IRA, self-proclaimed inheritors of the United Irishmen's mantle, left a firebomb in the library which destroyed several hundred books.

An Phoblacht, the republican movement's newspaper, reported the attack in an issue housed, like all previous issues, in the Linen Hall's political collection. A charitable person would say this was the Provos attempting to go post-modern, a terrorist version of the text that deconstructs itself.

Now I'm not one for claiming that destroying a couple of hundred rare books is worse than taking a single life, but I can think of few more eloquent examples of how intellectually bankrupt the IRA's campaign had become. Within nine months, that campaign was over. Six years on, Habitat has come, the Disney store has come, and where once there were none there are more Sainsbury's and Tescos than you could – in an entirely non-threatening way, you understand – shake a stick at. A new hotel opens every other week, we have a concert hall fronted entirely with glass, and now the Linen Hall has undergone a £3 million-plus expansion.

The makeover will be officially unveiled this weekend. There's bound to be a big turnout, including, I'm sure, a few people who the Special Branch at English airports probably fantasised about interviewing those years ago when they were examining the contents of my wallet: councillors and members of our Legislative Assembly now, and very good ones some of them are too.

Topping the bill is the man who brought the Nobel Prize to Northern Ireland and gained an extra surname, 'Seamus Heaney Himself'. The high point for me, though, will be the screening, in the new events room, of 'Snooker', a short film by young Belfast director Lab Ky Mo.

Travelling through Europe this summer, I heard someone say, in praise of its diversity, that Europe was very unlike itself. Long may the Linen Hall library stand as a reminder that Belfast can be very unlike itself too.

Night Waves, September 2000

Peace pause

Last Saturday, for the first time this spring, the sun shone. I went with my wife to buy a gift for my brother who has just bought one of the many new houses which are visible wherever you look these days in our city. We drove to a large home improvement store on the outskirts of town. Such were the crowds, the only space we could find to park was under a hoarding on which were announced plans to expand the store into the biggest home improvement outlet in the United Kingdom.

I was suddenly reminded of the cartoon characters, galloping off the edge of a cliff, not noticing that the ground has disappeared from beneath their feet. Could this really be *Belfast*, a mere month after the suspension of Northern Ireland's first devolved government for a quarter of a century?

Whether galloping off cliffs, or shopping and home improving, the trick to avoiding disaster, as everyone knows, is not to stop and think.

But maybe I am being too harsh. Maybe the shoppers I found myself among last Saturday afternoon knew it was the ground that briefly appeared beneath their feet – the devolved government – that was the illusion. Maybe after years of practice, there is nothing too dramatic-seeming about treading politically thin air once again.

Don't get me wrong, the vast majority of people here were enthusiastic about our ten weeks of devolution. Nobody I knew was looking forward to it coming to an end. At the same time, though, you can't help feeling that we have been here before: another March, another deadlock, another exodus of local politicians to Washington for the St Patrick's day celebrations and talks with the American president to move the process forward. *Crisis management* has become indistinguishable from actual government.

And yet there is a growing sense that this most recent difficulty has exposed divisions which the Good Friday Agreement never properly addressed, divisions which have, if anything, got wider in the intervening months. Depressingly, it's possible again to guess a person's religion by their views on certain issues. One who says that the weapons question will be resolved once power-sharing is restored is likely to be Catholic; one saying no more power-sharing until the weapons question is resolved is likely to be Protestant.

The holders of the weapons, meanwhile, the paramilitaries, continue to talk as though they are disciplined armies and act as though they are crazed biker gangs. At present, Protestant groups are feuding amongst themselves. As so often before, the violence, once started, quickly becomes indiscriminate.

Maybe this, more than anything, explains the queue of cars at the home improvement store; for the uglier things get on the streets, the greater is the temptation to retreat indoors. And, despite all its beautiful new houses, there are times just now when Northern Ireland can look very, very ugly indeed.

Swedish Broadcasting Corporation, March 2000

Take two (three, four, five...)

Well, it was a long time coming, but the first historic day of the Northern Irish political year dawned, and died, before the street lights came on. For all the careful choreography, the Unionists and Sinn Féin were not about to avoid treading on one another's toes.

I will own up here: I wrote a version of this in Belfast before catching an early evening plane to Luton, only to find when I switched on my mobile in arrivals that most of what I'd written was destined, like the hopes of an agreement, for the bin. The Belfast version imagined that this time they meant every word that they said – or at least every word they had led us to believe they had said. For that was one thing I noticed straight away. As historic days in the peace process go, yesterday was – media speculation aside – strangely muted.

I spent the morning at Queen's University teaching my undergraduate creative writing class. On the way home, I stopped at the bank, a garage and a shop. Not one person mentioned the morning's political developments. Nor was this a case of whatever you say, say nothing. If we weren't exactly dancing in the streets when the Good Friday Agreement was reached – the politicians had monopolised the choreography – we were at least talking, ringing friends, people who had once drunkenly scribbled their names on beer mats...

The Good Friday Agreement made us all feel like actors in the big picture. The talks of past days, involving only two of the local parties, added to the growing suspicion that most of us were only ever extras.

That Northern Ireland has changed for the better in the interim is everywhere apparent. The dead zone that was the city centre in the 1970s is contracting week by week. Stores that wouldn't have dreamed of moving here at the height of the conflict have come, and in some cases, gone. Forget post-ceasefire, we are living in the post-Habitat era now.

My new novel includes the line, 'Summer time is marching time, the time of bonfires, planned and improvised, and of nightly confrontations along (a popular summer term) the sectarian interfaces.' In fact, this summer was almost free of major sectarian incidents. On the very July day that I sent the manuscript to my publishers, a sculpture was unveiled at one of east Belfast's interfaces: a short wall mounted with the bronze face-masks of local Protestant and Catholic schoolchildren, which together spelled the word 'hope' in capitals.

Novels, of course, are not newspapers. Still, I was glad that day I had settled on the title *That Which Was*.

I suspect the majority of Northern Irish people were as quietly hopeful as I was that yesterday's announcements would be genuinely historic.

In the Belfast version, I urged them to go out and endorse them at next month's elections. At the same time, I noted that the morning news that announced those elections also brought word of the formal identification of Jean McConville, a widowed mother of ten murdered and secretly buried by the Belfast IRA more than thirty years ago. That which was, I wrote, still has questions to ask of that which is to be. Sadly, it seems, yet again too many.

The taxi driver taking me to the airport told me he had seen Concorde flying into Belfast earlier. 'Imagine,' he said, 'Concorde and the war over in the same day.' He paused. 'Well at least I can be sure of one of the two: I saw Concorde.' And I was still smiling at this when I touched down in Luton.

Guardian, October 2003

Belfast to Boston

'Sideburns', a Stranglers-inspired fanzine, once famously carried a cover showing the fretboard fingering for A, E and G. This is a chord, ran the caption. This is another. This is a third. Now form a band.

Somewhere, I can only imagine, there is a magazine with the following instructions. This is a whistly-sounding thing. This is an acoustic guitar. These – 'the rising of the moon', 'ancient hatred', 'long injustice', 'martyred fellows' – are lyrics. Now make a Belfast record. Mournfully.

James Taylor's 'Belfast to Boston' is as mournful as they come. Taylor doesn't attempt the accent but otherwise asks us to accept for two minutes and fifty-two seconds of whistly stuff, moon rising and unplugged guitar that he is not the multi-Grammy-award-winning ex-husband of Carly Simon, but a Belfast man sending a message across the Atlantic, possibly from one of the new riverside apartments with no intrusive traffic sounds, or possibly having waited till the wee small hours to allow five-hours-backwards

Boston time to get home from work and fix a drink. He has an important message to deliver, after all, better that Boston is relaxed, sitting down.

Boston, it's like this.... Well, Boston, you see – we appreciate your interest and everything, but... How do I put this?

Dontsendusanymoreguns.

Thanks.

And thank you, James. I'll not be churlish and say you're twenty frigging years too late. I'll go further and omit the frigging if this ever goes to a second edition. I'll even allow that your use of the tired old phrases quoted, to say nothing of 'the blessing of forgiveness' and 'take the devil for a countryman', makes this the perfect song for our peace process, which as the whole world knows we would only buy into (political juveniles that we are) if it was sold to us in language – *languages* – that didn't require us to ask too many hard questions of ourselves.

But, fuck it, guy, could you speed it up a bit, stop singing about us as though the City Hall was thatched?

Partly due to my own incompetence (the deadline looms, as ever I have been optimistic in thinking I could easily meet it), partly due to the dreadful torpor that descends on me each time I put this track in the CD tray and press play, I am writing this in Hiroshima: in a hotel room, to be precise, five hundred metres from the hypocentre of the atom bomb blast. Three hundred and eighty-five metres from the hypocentre is a bank, which somehow came through the blast more or less intact, though all around was totally levelled and forty-seven people inside were killed. (The bank opened for business two days later. Trams were running again in three.) Talk about putting things into perspective. Outside the toilets in a bar I was in on my first night here was a plastic bucket half-filled with coins. This, a Japanese friend explained to me, was for the *hibakusha*, the three hundred thousand survivors of the A-bomb. Who knows what manner of trauma the word 'survivor' masks?

Who knows why there are mournful Belfast songs by the yard and only 'Enola Gay' that springs to mind about the bomb that destroyed Hiroshima?

I am here as a guest of the quite wonderful Japan branch of IASIL, the International Association for the Study of Irish Literature, whose two hundred and fifty members travel for meetings the length and breadth of Japan. (It mightn't be that broad, but it's a long country, Japan; long, long, long.) Many of them attend the annual get-together of worldwide IASIL branches: last year Sao Paolo, next year Budapest. Not a few of them have spent time in Belfast. One member I have got to know well subscribes to *Fortnight*. I have talked to people about restaurants on the Lisburn Road, about the site of the old ropeworks in relation to Holywood Arches. They know their stuff. And yet, and yet. The musical entertainment at the opening night's party was a male voice choir singing (well, it has to be said) 'A Nation Once Again'. A tape deck in the foyer, meanwhile, burbles more or less non-stop with something Celtic and ethereal. And it occurs to me that rarely in any of the festivals or conferences I have attended have I heard anything that reflects the music that the majority of people where I come from buy, or for that matter the music that many of them have, with great distinction, energy and basic, thrilling *noise*, made over the last half a century. No jazz, no blues, no rock 'n' roll, no punk, no house, no techno.

Forget about the post-industrial society, in this one respect it's as though the industrial revolution never happened.

When Sonic Youth played the Belfast art college in 1991, they told on-stage how one of the things that turned them on when they were in their teens was John T. Davis's film about the Belfast punk scene, *Shellshocked Rock*. (As I recall, there were quite a few people in the audience who had been in bands featured in the film.) It made them, they said, realise that there were people out there in the world just like them. They may even have said it helped save them. And I thought what a pleasant change it was for Belfast at last to have provided the soundtrack for a different sort of romantic projection. And then, too, I knew just what Sonic Youth meant. I felt much the same way when I first heard 'Roadrunner' by Jonathan Richman, born in Boston three years and a musical generation after James Taylor. I was sure music like this would save all of us. No hanging around waiting for paramilitaries to be prodded into embracing politics (paramilitaries? for politicians themselves to embrace it); or for James Taylor records, for that matter.

How could anyone with ears to hear a song that included the words 'modern' and 'love' over and over and over (Richman's band was the Modern Lovers, even the moonlight in 'Roadrunner' was modern), how could anyone who heard that get their head around killing someone over religion or nationality or ethnicity or driving a taxi or mending the roof of an army barracks?

Oh, well. What did I know?

By the time I saw Jonathan Richman live, in the Limelight, November 2000, I was a rough quarter of a century older and none the wiser. We had a six-year-old peace whose goodness was in danger of being processed right out of it. We had beatings and shootings and pipe bombings. We had parity of esteem and victimhood, which sometimes seemed to mean only that none our doleful readings of the last thirty years were to be subject to scrutiny or challenge. I still thought what this city needed was someone yelping about being in love with rock 'n' roll and being out all night.

I still think it.

Stuff the rising of the moon, give me modern moonlight every time.

Belfast to Boston, keep James Taylor, send us Jonathan Richman back.

Belfast Songs, November 2002

Be(lfa)st boy

George Best was almost too good to be true. If a writer had invented him, critics would, with some justification, have poured scorn on his near-perfection. There is that name, for a start. In this century perhaps only Elvis (rhymes with pelvis, lives, anagrammatically, always) comes close in appearing to have been born into a name that matched his destiny. At his peak, George was better than best — no less a person than the previous best, Pele, said it. So much better that they had to coin a new superlative: Bestie.

Or consider his timing. Born nine months after VJ Day, in the first full year of what has passed for half a century of world peace, he was the quintessential baby boomer, coming of age in that apogee of post-war optimism, the Sixties.

Even the place where he grew up seems significant. Before he had properly found his feet, his family had removed from Donard Street, off Belfast's Ravenhill Road, to the Cregagh Estate. In its then semi-rural setting, Cregagh was in every respect a step away from the narrow terraces with which Belfast in the popular imagination was traditionally associated. Walking around the estate fifty years later, it is still possible to appreciate the improved standards of layout and design that it represented, possible, too, to believe that even in a Northern Ireland resistant to the burgeoning welfare state, the war's end had engendered a reinvigorated spirit of municipalism.

That there was a new mood abroad in those years is incontestable. Labour's 1945 election landslide held out the promise that in the future success would depend on ability, not station. George Best would become the second most potent symbol of that myth, after a quartet of other northern provincials to whose careers Best's own seemed on occasion to be index-linked. Three of the Beatles (the exception was Ringo Starr) were working-class suburbanites like Best. Like Best, it was not only their talent which set them apart from their predecessors. Despite the 'safe' collarless suits which their manager, Brian Epstein, obliged them to wear, the Beatles were almost effortlessly iconoclastic. The impact of 'She Loves You' in summer 1963 has been attributed in part to the British public's disillusionment with the drawn-out Profumo affair and the whiff of corruption emanating from the Macmillan government. The group's follow-up, 'I Want to Hold Your Hand', was released in November that same year, on the back of a triumphant appearance at the Royal Command Performance, when John Lennon famously enjoined patrons in the dear seats to rattle their jewellery in time to the music. In December, George Best scored on his second appearance for Manchester United.

He had arrived in England two years before, a slight

fifteen-year-old who had never until then been further from his Belfast home than Bangor. Homesick, he returned to the Cregagh Estate after twenty-four hours, and was enticed back only with great difficulty.

If popular music – the whole of what would soon be called popular culture – was undergoing seismic change as the Sixties began, the same was true of association football. The abolition of the £20 maximum wage in 1961 began the gradual detachment of 'the people's game' from the broad mass of working-class men who had traditionally filled its professional ranks and terraces alike. Football was about to be transformed from a well-paid trade into a business in which young fit males could earn huge financial rewards. There had been fame and adulation before, of course, and Denis Compton had already opened up another lucrative sideline by appearing in Bryl-creem ads, but after 1961, British football was just waiting for its first superstar. Best, scorer of six first-team goals before his eighteenth birthday, more than fit the bill. And Manchester United, managed by Matt Busby, already had two claims on the hearts of the wider British public. Their Old Trafford ground had had to be rebuilt after damage sustained in the Blitz and half of their finest post-war side, the 'Busby Babes', had been wiped out in the Munich air disaster of 1958. That Best was truly gifted, blessed perhaps, was not incidental, but the deification (or should that be reification?) depended on a combination of factors beyond even his legendary control. Television undoubtedly helped accelerate the process. It was no longer necessary to be in the stadium, nor even to rely on the curiously atmosphere-free Pathé newsreels, to keep up with the game. Football was reaching worldwide audiences.

When United went to Portugal in March 1966 and destroyed Benfica in the European Cup quarter finals, Best, who notched two of their five goals, became an international celebrity. It was after this game that the English press went the final step and dubbed him El Beatle. Other people could claim him all they liked, however; in the words of the Don Fardon song, 'Georgie' was still a 'Belfast Boy' and never more so than when leaving other, preferably English, players floundering in his wake.

For the people of Northern Ireland especially, Best was part of what the Sixties were all about. He was in a sense our representative in Swinging Britain, as exotic as nightclubs and Miss Worlds, as reassuring as the Cookstown sausages he advertised on our televisions; though – the way he winked before taking a bite – it was clear nobody could have more fun with a sausage than George. Sex *was* an important part of the equation. Van Morrison aside, Belfast had yet to produce a pop-star in the true sense of the term, and in any case Van Morrison never got you where you most wanted to be got when you were young, below the belt. With Best, on the other hand, there were only two possible responses: you either wanted to be him or shag him. He was the subject of the first risqué song I ever learnt:

Georgie Best, superstar,
Wears frilly knickers and a Playtex bra.
The bra's too big, he wears a wig,
That's why they call him a sexy pig.

Note the easy substitution of Georgie Best for the Jesus Christ of the original. Note, too, at eight, bra was a formidable word.

I had a friend who used to kiss his George Best badge before going to sleep at night. I myself had a three-feet-high poster (won in a Boys' Brigade competition) of Best, in full flight, on the back of my bedroom door. I loved that poster. I loved George.

I only ever got to see him once in the flesh, against England at Windsor Park when I was nine years old. My father, a sheet-metal worker, had made me a stool to stand on for an adult's-eye view of the match. We were on the terraces before the main stand, a little to the right of the England dug-out: the perfect position from which to observe the moment when, with the score still 0-0, the England goalkeeper, Gordon Banks, tossed the ball in the air to clear up-field only for Best to flick it over his head and then nod it into the empty net. I jumped so high I missed the stool as I came down. By the time my father had righted me again the referee had awarded a free-kick against Best and the goal was disallowed. England won the game 1-0.

I wish I could say, for the sake of irony, that I comforted myself with the thought that there would be another year, but a year then seemed to me forever away. Looking back on it now, though, it is difficult not to see in that moment of thwarted brilliance the beginning of the end of something.

It was May 1971. Not just George Best but things in general were about to get hairier and heavier.

In the autumn of that year Best failed to turn up for a Northern Ireland game. There was talk at the time of an IRA death threat, though the talk was more often about the star's worsening drink problem. Suddenly there weren't too many reasons to feel good about being Northern Irish. 'Best AWOL' headlines soon became commonplace. The 'fifth' Beatle, it seemed, was going the way of the other four.

The group's split had become official early in 1970. By May 1971 Paul McCartney had released his second solo album, *Ram*, described by *Rolling Stone* as 'the nadir in the decomposition of Sixties rock thus far.' I stress, *rock*. Rock 'n' roll, a joyous euphemism for fucking, had grown weighty and self-indulgent. Football, too, was entering something of a bloated rock-star stage. The manager of the moment was no longer Manchester United's Matt Busby, but Manchester City's Malcolm Allison, all cigars, champagne and fedoras. 'Fat' Franny Lee, penalty expert (earning and taking), was City's leading goalscorer. There was a feeling of excess, even as crowds declined and rival fans rioted. By the time Denis Law, transferred from United to City in the 1973 close season, scored at Old Trafford to send his former club down to the second division and spark bon-fires on the Stretford End, Best had left United for good, an alcoholic whose self-destruction seemed to me, a twelve-year-old fan following the story on television, to mirror Northern Ireland's own. This is not to trivialise matters. All that I remembered as good in my childhood had turned bad. In five years, one thousand people had been killed in Northern Ireland, the vast majority of them since 1971. (Northern Ireland, as a consequence, were obliged to play their 'home' international matches in England.) A week after the 1973–4 season's end, the Ulster Workers' Council strike began.

The Seventies got worse. Best began an odyssey around lower-division clubs and the American cabaret-soccer circuit. There were occasional highlights; there were also stomach implants to stop him drinking (they didn't), there were brawls and fines and eventually there was a six-week jail term. At the end of the decade, ITV pundits gallingly –

gleefully, I always thought – voted the workmanlike and, let's be frank, un-sexy Kevin Keegan the better of the two players.

New Bests had been proclaimed as often as new Beatles. But Peter Marinello was as convincing in his role as the Bay City Rollers were in theirs; we briefly let ourselves mistake the hype, the hair and the grins for the real thing.

The feeling grew that perhaps only the arrival at maturity of a generation who had no first-hand experience of either would dispel what was clearly becoming a tedious nostalgia.

Some might say that has now happened. British football, like British pop, was transformed in the early 1990s. United in particular have been thriving ever since. In Ryan Giggs they have a player who on his top form (which is not often enough for the comparison to be pushed) is as thrilling to watch as Best was, in David Beckham a player as capable of making the headlines front page and back.

Northern Ireland qualified for two consecutive World Cups in the Eighties, something they never managed with Best in the team, and currently have a halfway decent side watched by crowds of under ten thousand. I am sometimes among them, as old now as my father was when Best stole the ball from Gordon Banks. It has come to be generally accepted that the 'goal' he scored that day ought to have stood. Best knew what the referee apparently did not, that the ball was in play from the moment it left the keeper's hands.

Best himself is almost fifty-one. He looks how I suppose a lot of us here in Northern Ireland feel: we have had a pretty ropy couple of decades and we're not completely out of the woods yet. He looks a bit like the man who used to be the greatest footballer the world has ever seen, which is no bad thing to look like, when all's said and done.

Causeway Magazine, Summer 1997

Stand up for the Ulstermen

I am, for my unglamorous sins, a Northern Ireland fan. That's Northern Ireland as in Northern Ireland 0, Everywhere Else 3.

Supporting Northern Ireland has its problems, the results apart. Take the name. For seventy years a significant number of people here have refused to acknowledge such a place as Northern Ireland exists. It is The North, to them, or the Six Counties.

Then there is the image problem.

Northern Ireland supporters, especially in the Kop end of Windsor Park, are...well, sectarian, frankly.

For years their musical repertoire has been drawn from the tunes thudded out every summer by Orange bands: 'The Sash', 'Derry's Walls' and the infamous 'Billy Boys', with its shaming chorus of 'up to our necks in Fenian blood'.

I normally go to matches with a novelist friend. He is a Catholic, in the same way that I am a Protestant, by the

106

accident of birth. More than once we have left the ground thoroughly sickened, vowing never to return. But, if you know Irish League soccer, you will know that internationals are our only chance of seeing proper football. And then, *we live here.* However problematic the allegiance, Northern Ireland is our team too.

So, last week, Switzerland came and we bought tickets. (At least, we thought, it would be an interesting clash of political systems.) That lunchtime Radio Ulster's *Talk Back* programme had been discussing whether Protestants were more bigoted than Catholics. It hadn't raised my spirits.

This was Northern Ireland's first international since the Good Friday Agreement, their second under manager Lawrie McMenemy. I had missed McMenemy's first match in charge, against Slovakia. A game Northern Ireland *won.* So, perhaps the song I heard sung as the teams took the field had been sung then, but it was new to me.

'Stand Up For the Ulstermen,' the Kop sang, to the tune of Oo-aa Eric Cantona, or 'Go West' by the very un-loyalist Village People.

It was quite rousing. Of course, nationalists would no more accept the name Ulster than they would Northern Ireland. The province of Ulster, they point out, has nine counties, three of them, temporarily, resident in the Republic. But still, 'Stand Up for the Ulstermen' was, we agreed, not the worst we had heard.

In fact, though we braced ourselves for the worst throughout the first half, the worst never came. There was the odd outbreak of 'The Sash', but it was not taken up with much conviction. Again and again, though, 'Stand Up for the Ulstermen' rang out. And the Kop stood, while we sat and secretly wished we were on our feet too.

I have only once heard someone rebuked for sectarian chanting at Windsor Park. 'That's enough,' he was told. It was ten minutes after kick-off. 'Save that for the second half.'

And they say bigotry is unthinking.

Sure enough, last Wednesday, the second half began with the 'Billy Boys', sung, I would swear, in response to a wave from the Northern Ireland manager as he trotted to the dug-out.

They must have thought he would like it.

Until recently our manager really was a Billy from Belfast. The song must have seemed particularly apt. But sung to Lawrie from Sunderland... ? Abruptly – miraculously – it stopped.

Instead the Kop took up another old favourite: 'Here Lies a Soldier'. The soldier referred to is a member of the Protestant terror group, the UVF, whose initials in the song resound like gunshots. You don't have to be Catholic to be intimidated.

So why wasn't I this time? Well, the PUP – the Progressive Unionist Party – which represents the UVF *supports* the Good Friday Agreement. In a recent poll, the PUP's leader, David Ervine, scored higher on credibility, with Protestants *and* Catholics, than any politician bar John Hume. The PUP has condemned the Loyalist Volunteer Force, who have carried on killing, and castigated Ian Paisley's Democratic Unionist Party for its rejection of the deal.

Earlier last week, in east Belfast, an area usually considered diehard loyalist, I had seen this graffiti: 'Defeat the DUP-LVF treachery. Vote YES [in the referendum].'

Thinking about this in Windsor Park, I saw a familiar face a few rows away. David Ervine's deputy, Billy

Hutchinson; Billy Hutchinson, a former soldier – as the song would have it – of the UVF who served sixteen years for murder; Billy Hutchinson, who I had last seen in the New Year at a rally in Belfast city centre protesting at the murders of eight Catholics; Billy Hutchinson sitting with his son. I don't know if the UVF song faded, like the 'Billy Boys', or if I simply stopped hearing it.

I came round to the strains of 'Blue Moon': 'Brazil, you should be watching, Brazil.'

Northern Ireland won, incidentally, by the game's only goal. Two wins in succession. We call that a run here.

At full-time, the Kop chanted 'One-nil to the Ulstermen'. The Ulstermen, who include, in these days of flexible nationality, a Nigerian, a German, several Englishmen and a Scot, applauded the crowd. And I stood. And my friend stood. Walking home, we were still singing and laughing at ourselves.

Imagining days ahead when it would be less of a problem to say you supported Northern Ireland.

Night Waves, April 1998

Billy bhoy

Christmas 1969. Northern Ireland had come through a very bad year. Even so, it was still possible to imagine that our troubles might quickly run their course. Or so I've been told. I was not yet very good on the long-term then. I was only eight years old. I still believed in Santa Claus. Confusing him with God, or perhaps thinking that was where he went to get his 'who's been good, who's been bad list', I eschewed the traditional note up the chimney and prayed instead for my Christmas presents. And prayed and prayed and prayed.

I wanted – I got – a football kit. Not just any football kit, mind you. In those far-off, 100% cotton days before sponsorship and manufacturer's branding, when a blue or a red, or even a black and white striped jersey could represent any number of teams, the kit I had asked for was entirely individual: white with emerald green hoops... I mean even saying that word, 'hoops'. How beautiful is that?

Oh, Celtic, I loved you.

So much did I support Glasgow Celtic that I also supported their Cork namesakes in the Republic's League of Ireland. Had I been born twenty years earlier, I dare say I would have supported Belfast Celtic too in our own Northern Irish League. But by the time I was growing up that club's Celtic Park stadium, off the Falls Road, was already a semi-derelict dog track. Belfast Celtic had been wound up after serious sectarian rioting at a match with their great rivals Linfield, whose Windsor Park ground, in the staunchly Protestant 'Village' area, was visible across the Bog Meadow from Celtic Park. Linfield's colours were, from the socks up, red, white and blue. Their policy on signing players was the subject of a song, popular in my childhood, by Ulster comic James Young: 'I'm the only Catholic on the Linfield team.' Linfield in those days made Rangers look like happy-clappy ecumenicists.

At Christmas 1969, when I was praying for my Celtic kit, I was a Linfield season ticket holder. I was as distinctive in my way as a green and white hooped jersey. I was a Billy Bhoy.

My parents were not stupid or reckless people. They would hardly have allowed God to tell Santa to bring me my Celtic kit if they had thought it was likely to get me into bother. Like I say, it was still possible in late 1969 to imagine our troubles would soon end. In fact, the only concern expressed for my well-being in relation to that kit was by my mother, who suspected me, correctly as it happens, of deliberately rolling around in the muck out on the football pitch. A muddy kit I thought looked more authentic.

Young and all as I was, and rolling in puddles aside, I wasn't entirely foolish either. I think I understood that for neatness if not my future health it would make sense to twin my support for Linfield with support for Rangers. There was one major drawback. Celtic were fucking magic. The first match I can remember seeing on television was Celtic's victory in the 1967 European Cup Final the year before my other great love, my English love, Manchester United won the trophy for the first time. (My *main* English love, I should say; I was promiscuous with my football affections and followed a team in each of the four English divisions. This only ended in 1974–5 when United found themselves, along with the other three clubs, in the old second division.) True, Celtic would lose to Feyenoord in the final of the 1970 European Cup, but having defeated Leeds United along the way in the so-called Battle of Britain, they were still undisputed kings of the domestic game. Why wouldn't I want to support them? Besides, I had a big brother who was Celtic daft, I could read his books, borrow his badges. He was even saving up to go across to Glasgow to see the Bhoys play.

I can no longer be certain, but I think it was when my brother returned from this very trip that the disenchantment set in. I am clear, though, that it was connected to the flying of the Irish tricolour at the ground. You must remember that, European games excepted, we almost never had the opportunity to see Celtic on TV back then. In fact, we saw more of Millwall and Crystal Palace, since Ulster Television took its Sunday match from London Weekend Television. So, sure, we knew all about – and could live with – the Catholic tag, but the flag appeared to identify the club explicitly with Irish nationalism; Irish nationalism's dearest wish was the dismantling of the state of Northern Ireland. These were dark days – the UDA by now was going through its paces on the football pitches outside our house, several Catholic families had already left the neighbourhood – it is perhaps not surprising our view was a little dim. We were fans of Northern Ireland, me and my brother, on the pitch and off. Catholicism we could live with, but this was an altogether higher order of paradox.

I had outgrown my Celtic kit. The next kit I asked my parents for (I had outgrown praying to Santa Claus too) was Manchester United's. Red with a white inset collar.

I tried to forget I had once been a Celtic fan, tried for a while supporting (quick, I can only think I told myself, pick a team at random) Dundee United. In the later Seventies I made a number of eccentric changes of allegiance – to Morton (for Andy Ritchie), then to Partick (for their colourful shirts) and even to Meadowbank Thistle (for John Peel, who also supported them) – and in the end, I gave up on Scottish football altogether. Apart, that is, from secretly wishing every week that Rangers would lose.

I was in any case living in England by this time; Scottish football wasn't exactly high profile. It wasn't until I returned to live in Northern Ireland in the early 1990s that I was reacquainted with the passions that the Scottish game aroused. Or rather, the passions that Celtic and Rangers aroused. Perhaps I had spent too long away, but it seemed to me that the rivalry had become much more overt. Or perhaps it was just that the wearing of replica jerseys had spread onto the high street from the public parks, to which it was still confined when I was in my teens.

And boy, had it ever spread. One of my nephews and two of my teenage nieces wore Rangers shirts; they wore, too, pendants in the shape of the club crest. They had entire catalogues of Rangers merchandise.

Considering the prominence given to the Ulster connection in recent years by Andy Goram and the 'dummy fluter' himself, Paul Gascoigne, it might seem a typically Protestant choice of team for them to make. In all likelihood, though, they support Rangers for the same reason that I supported Celtic when I was young: they are by far and away the best team in Scotland. (Alas for Scottish football, however, best in Scotland is hardly a term to make the world quake any more.) My nephew and my nieces look faintly bemused when I tell them about my childhood passion. It is not a religious matter. I think they feel pity towards me. The same pity they evince when I declare that my favourite Northern Irish team is now Lisburn Distillery, though in fact I frequently forget these days even to listen out for the local scores.

I haven't attended an Irish League match since the mid-Eighties, when I was a student, home on Christmas holiday. Linfield *v* Bangor. The football was utterly appalling, the chanting and flag-waving from the sparsely populated terraces hardly less so. Once you step outside, it's hard to step back in. By the same token, even though I am once more surrounded by Scottish football, too long a time has elapsed for me to work up the old enthusiasm for Celtic. I don't know the players' names, I don't even much care for the restyled kit.

Given the frustrations of the past decade and more, however, and given my twenty-year wait for Man United to come good again, I am not entirely sorry.

Perhaps supporting Celtic really would have been injurious to my health. The potential hazard was summed up for me the year before last by a long-time Celtic-supporting friend who told me his brother had suffered a non-fatal heart attack during another lost Old Firm match.

'God,' I said, 'that's awful.'

'I'll tell you what's awful,' said my friend. 'I was conscious the entire game.'

August 2000

Cigs

These are – I know the rest of the world might take some convincing – interesting times in Belfast. Last week a member of the CBI here declared that we were no longer in a peace process, but a political process. Sinn Féin and the Democratic Unionist Party – the nightmare ticket of last year's assembly elections – are, many commentators reckon, a matter of weeks from an agreement that will see them in government together. The DUP leader, Ian Paisley, who forty years ago threw snowballs at the first Irish premier to visit Belfast, recently travelled to Dublin to meet the current taioseach, Bertie Ahern.

In that semi-metaphorical – no, make that semi-*mythical* – place 'the streets', meanwhile, change is every bit as marked.

Earlier this year the Shankill Road picked up a Keep Britain Tidy Award in recognition of efforts to remove dozens of paramilitary murals and the red, white and blue paint from several thousand yards of kerbstones. Murals, in fact, are starting to look distinctly last century. Bad news, that, for the mural decoding industry, of which I confess I have been an occasional employee. We are entering into the *memorial* era. All over the city, gardens of remembrance are sprouting up, with plaques and obelisks to the glorious fallen. The word from republican quarters is that campaign medals have already been struck, that a standing down of the Provisional IRA could be ordered for early spring. Before that we are being primed to expect a fourth, definitive act of decommissioning, or, should I say (for as with 'standing down' the terminology is all-important), of 'putting arms beyond use'.

All of which makes certain recent events here the more curious. For it seems there is one deadly addiction that the Provisionals have yet to try to break.

Early last month £2 million worth of cigarettes were stolen from a Belfast industrial estate. Almost at once there were allegations of IRA involvement. Certainly the scale of the operation, which involved taking a family hostage, called to mind the robbery, near the border, this time last year in which a twelve-man gang held the driver of a lorry for *questioning* before relieving him of his cargo of cigarettes. After that robbery the Dublin government's justice minister declared that not only were the IRA up to their necks in criminality, but that the proceeds helped to fund Sinn Féin. Sinn Féin accused him of electioneering. Bertie Ahern issued a quick retraction: yes the IRA were involved in criminality, but no Sinn Féin were not beneficiaries, which was maybe just as well, given that he was due in Downing Street the next day to meet a Sinn Féin delegation and a British Prime Minister whose Exchequer had just been left several hundred thousand pounds lighter.

In fact, as long ago as December 2001, after still another cigarette heist, the *Sunday Times* Ireland correspondent Liam Clarke reported that the IRA had set up a unit tasked with large-scale robberies to break the Sinn Féin dependence on funds from America, at that time depressed by a combination of the 9/11 effect and alleged IRA involvement in Colombia.

Maybe, with such accusations never far from the surface, the remarkable thing is that the political process has got even this far. There is a feeling, though (you may have heard it from Gerry Adams here on *Night Waves* a few weeks ago), that it is bad form to carp: at least things aren't as bad as they used to be. So what if the names on your local UVF war memorial include that of a suspected mass murderer? So what if medals are handed out to the IRA gang who invented the suicide-bomb-by-proxy when they strapped Patsy Gillespie into the cab of his explosives-laden lorry and pointed it at an army checkpoint? If there is going to be an end by Easter, isn't this all a small price to pay?

Probably, yes.

But then again.

The week before last a seminar at Queen's University reported that loyalist and republican paramilitary organisations had between them beaten twenty-two males below the age of seventeen in the past year. The organisers of the seminar – the Institute of Irish Studies and Save the Children – were seeking to have these offences designated as child abuse. The near silence with which this call was met, even within Northern Ireland, is all the more alarming when you hear it suggested that IRA members without previous convictions might – post-stand-down – be admitted into our restructured and supposedly reformed police service.

(And there I was thinking the idea was to *get rid of* the human rights abuses.)

Oh, and on the subject of those IRA members...the Provisionals at the time of their 1994 ceasefire were reckoned to have about six hundred active members. Assuming no dramatic increase in membership in the last decade and assuming, too, that not all are heavy smokers, you have to ask what they want with all those missing cigarettes, or indeed with the proceeds from their sale. If you buy the Bertie Ahern line about Sinn Féin and if you rule out the possibility of *re*commissioning – 'bringing arms back within reach' – then all you can conclude is that we are soon going to see some pretty state-of-the-art ex-active-servicemen's (and -women's) huts next to our gardens of paramilitary remembrance.

If you ask me, though, the Provisionals should forget about medals for the time being and stick to patches.

Night Waves, November 2004

The people's army loves the people

The IRA will not decommission, it says, because it is an army 'undefeated in the field'. (An archaic phrase and, given the way the IRA has conducted much of its campaign, a not spectacularly accurate one.) Not only is it an undefeated army, it is, as Eamonn McCann has previously pointed out on these pages, Óglaigh na hÉireann, *the* Irish army. Never mind for the moment what the army of the state of the Republic of Ireland thinks of this, the IRA's logic runs thus: the British army couldn't beat our army, so our army doesn't have to give up its guns unless and until it wants to.

In fact, though, if the IRA really does want to be considered an army, then it has a greater than ever obligation to begin disarming immediately. Despite attempts by Sinn Féin to portray decommissioning as a Unionist-fashioned stick to beat them with, it is virtually incontestable that the majority of people north and south desire the destruction or handing in of weapons. True, very many republicans (though not necessarily all) do not want to see any change in the IRA stance. Sinn Féin might argue that the people who voted for them did so knowing that it was their policy not to force decommissioning on a reluctant IRA. (Not to twist their own arms, you might almost say.) Sinn Féin, however, is the only political party on the island which is not now calling for guarantees on decommissioning. When Seamus Mallon urged action at the end of January, Sinn Féin responded, ominously, that the Deputy First Minister's thinking on the matter had always been 'wrong' and suggested that Mallon's party leader, John Hume, represented the right-thinking mind of the SDLP. Last week, however, Hume himself called for the symbolic destruction of a quantity of semtex. 'I now appeal to the IRA,' Hume wrote in the *Irish News*, 'to show their deep respect for the will of the Irish people. I ask them to demonstrate for all to see their patriotism.'

Cut through the characteristically flattering language, with which it appears the IRA is currently to be addressed, and the message is unambiguous.

All armies should be accountable to the democratically elected institutions of the state and, by extension, to the people those institutions represent and serve. It is, in this regard, an ongoing disgrace that so many killings by members of the British army in Northern Ireland have gone unpunished. The new inquiry into Bloody Sunday, though belated, is to be welcomed and all attempts to limit its reach are to be vigorously opposed. There is, however, a curious double standard in republican circles. If the British Army can be capable of crimes, then why can't the self-styled Irish Army be also? Yet many of the IRA's methods (e.g. torture of suspected informers, indiscriminate civilian bombing) have clearly infringed international standards of human rights and the conduct of war. How, in moral terms, does the shooting of an off-duty part-time soldier differ from the shooting of an unarmed IRA volunteer? Again, morally speaking, is Bloody Friday any less of a war crime than Bloody Sunday?

Can it really be the height of republican ambition to be 'no worse than anybody else'?

Yet the lengths to which the Provisionals went to ensure there could be no legal comeback on them before releasing even the flimsiest information on the whereabouts of the 'Disappeared' (victims of extrajudicial execution, at best) shows how little they care for scrutiny. Being a Provo clearly means never having to explain yourself. Forget no worse, when it comes to accountability these days, the IRA are the worst of all.

The idea that an army can be answerable only to one party or, worse still, answerable to no democratically elected party whatever, carries very ugly, totalitarian connotations.

In fact, the IRA's continuing disregard for the wishes of the people of this island calls to mind nothing so much as the slogan broadcast from tanks rolling into Tiananmen Square during the assault on pro-democracy demonstrators: 'The People's Army loves the People'.

The IRA continues to give the impression that it would rather love us all to death than give up its guns.

Either that, of course, or it's not really an army at all, just a couple of hundred people scared of the vagaries of democracy where force of argument alone does not always get you everything you want.

Belfast Telegraph, February 2000

Ask me another one

Two months into the IRA ceasefire – two months down the semantic road from complete to permanent, and with the loyalists now thankfully in tow – people in Northern Ireland are beginning to take some sort of definitive stock. Too many people, of all political beliefs, or no beliefs at all, have suffered in the past twenty-five years for relief not to be tempered by a more reflective mood. There is no doubt that the cost of the violence in Northern Ireland, in human terms, has been enormous – though talking recently to a Sri Lankan bishop on a fact-finding visit to Belfast I was reminded again how much worse things might have been here, if for instance the death rate had remained throughout at its 1972–3 level. The cost in other terms, however, might be longer in reckoning, or even indeed in expressing.

For one of the most serious casualties of the conflict, I would suggest, has been language itself. It has suffered from sustained and systematic attempts at silencing oppositional voices, whether enforced by government decree or terrorist bullet; it has suffered from euphemism and the mealy-mouthed condemnations of the apologists of violence; it has suffered from propaganda and not infrequently from out-and-out lies.

Truth in Northern Ireland has been so devalued that double-talk long ago ceased to be thought remarkable. In the hyper-inflationary culture of disinformation, quadruple- and even quintuple-talk appeared in recent years to have become common currency. At the same time, words appropriated to particular causes were stripped of the sub-tlety that gives language its real vitality, its sense of *possibility*. Identity was reduced to one thing or the other, Protestant or Catholic; dead words, tit-for-tat words, words to settle scores by.

Nothing, it seemed, was immune. Justice in one mouth was a system which flouted European conventions on human rights; justice in another sanctioned the maiming of adolescents and the expulsion of people from their homes. (And it is worth remembering that in this respect the cease-fire has not brought much of an improvement in the record of either the British government – John Major's Europa Hotel speech notwithstanding – or the Provisionals.) Even the word 'peace', as the past months have shown, was rendered suspect.

Little wonder, then, that this was a society where taci-turnity was elevated to a cardinal virtue: *Whatever you say, say nothing.*

But if peace is to be real and lasting, if peace is to amount to more than simply the old enmities without the guns, as many people as possible here are going to have to say something and say it soon. We have, in short, got to start making language work for us, expressing who we are and how we live, empowering rather than imprisoning us. This act, in effect, of reclamation necessitates us looking again at words which for political reasons we have been denied or made to feel uncomfortable with.

Take a simple example. Take the word 'No'.

Now I was born a Protestant; I grew up in a unionist household and came to political awareness, in the early Seventies, in an environment which was increasingly loyalist. My defence of the negative might seem to some entirely predictable. In the sectarian sociolinguistics of our island, no is what northern Protestants say best.

But there's no and there's no.

There is the no – heard here for far too long – that refuses any change, that resists self-scrutiny, and there is the no whose very denial contains the germ of an alternative affirmation, that is, the first step to yes. Only by rejecting that which artificially divides us can we clear the ground on which to begin the positive task of building a truly equitable society.

Again, though, care is required in the choice of words used to carry forward the debate. It will not do, for example, to continue referring to the 'unionist community', as though that term encompasses all those who are, by the accident of birth, Protestant. (My own view on the act of union, for what it's worth, has always been that it is a beautiful thing for two people in love to perform.) Still less will it do to carry on talking blithely about the 'Protestant tradition'. *Which* tradition is that exactly? The tradition of Roaring Hanna and Ian Paisley, or the tradition of the eighteenth-century Belfast radicals who founded the United Irishmen?

The same criticism, of course, could – *should* – be made of the terms 'nationalist' and 'Catholic', indeed of any language that obscures the true multiplicity of experience and outlook here in Northern Ireland.

And can I be certain that such a process will ensure a definite end to the bitterness of the past twenty-five years?

In a word, no.

All I know for sure is that if we keep on asking the questions in the same old ways (and, despite the silence of the guns, many of the old questions *are* still being asked), it should come as no surprise if all we keep on hearing in return are the same old answers.

Observer, October 1994

McCartney sisters

Magennis's Bar is a good indicator of how Belfast has changed in the eleven years since the first IRA ceasefire. Five minutes' walk from the City Hall, with a handsome 1920s façade, it is a bar you would go into without a second thought in any other city. In Belfast, though, small distances hide big divides. In the past many people would have viewed Magennis's as close to the strongly nationalist Markets district, rather than close to the city centre. Post-ceasefire, however, the area around the bar has undergone major redevelopment. The Hilton Hotel opened on the edge of the river Lagan, within sight of Magennis's front door, and the bar was popular with people of all backgrounds going to concerts at the new Waterfront Hall, next door to the Hilton.

So when, on Monday, 31 January this year, the morning news reported that a thirty-three-year-old man had died after being stabbed outside Magennis's the night before, it was a tremendous shock. Even so, there was nothing to suggest that the name of the victim, Robert McCartney, would linger long in the public's mind. Knife-crime has been increasing in Northern Ireland, as has what is sometimes referred to as 'ordinary murder', to distinguish it from the politically motivated killings of the recent past.

That Monday evening, riots erupted as police carried out searches in the Markets. The word was they were looking for a 'senior republican', code for 'leading IRA member'. Even this was not too unusual. Republicans, senior as well as junior, have been responsible for numerous deaths since the ceasefire. In 1998, Andrew Kearney, also thirty-three, was shot and left to bleed to death in north Belfast after allegedly beating a well-known IRA man in a fist fight. There had been uproar, calls for sanctions against Sinn Féin, but only for a time.

After the rioting in the Markets, Sinn Féin accused the police of heavy-handedness. The senior republican was released without charge and, once again, it seemed as though Robert McCartney's murder, like Andrew Kearney's, might soon be forgotten.

The reason it wasn't was summed up in an *Observer* news-paper headline two weekends later. 'Grieving Sisters Square Up to IRA.' The report, written by Henry McDonald, who himself grew up in the Markets, was the first graphic account of what happened in Magennis's on 30 January. Many of the seventy or so customers that night were IRA and Sinn Féin members who had just returned from Derry, where they had taken part in a march to commemorate the thirty-third anniversary of Bloody Sunday, when British paratroops shot dead fourteen unarmed demonstrators at an anti-internment rally. Robert McCartney, from nearby Short Strand, and his friend Brendan Devine happened to

be in the bar too. They got into an argument with some of
the IRA men, whose leader, according to the *Observer*, made
a stabbing motion: the signal for a savage assault that began
inside the bar and carried on out on the street. Robert
McCartney was not simply stabbed; he was slashed, beaten
with metal sewer rods and had his head jumped on with
such force he lost an eye. Brendan Devine somehow survived, despite having his throat cut and being ripped from
navel to neck by his assailant's knife. Hard as it is to believe,
no one in the bar appeared to have seen anything.

Robert McCartney's sisters – Gemma, Paula, Catherine,
Donna, Claire – and Bridgeen Hagans, mother of his two
young sons, certainly found it hard to believe. They were con-
vinced the IRA was intimidating witnesses. By refusing to be
intimidated themselves and calling on anyone with information to contact the police, the sisters were challenging not just
the IRA, but Sinn Féin, which has insisted that the new Police
Service of Northern Ireland is still unacceptable to Catholics.
For Paula McCartney, the issue was simple: 'If they get away
with Robert's murder,' she said, 'they will think they can get
away with anything and that would be really scary.'

The really scary truth is that for a considerable period
after the ceasefires it seemed as though 'they' thought they
could indeed get away with anything, including (as the case
of Andrew Kearney shows) murder. All the historic statements, presidential visits and Nobel Peace Prizes of recent
years have glossed over the fact that substantial parts of
Northern Ireland are effectively controlled by loyalist and
republican paramilitaries. So while Sinn Féin negotiated
with the British government for an amnesty for 'on-the-run'
IRA prisoners, the IRA itself was still exiling people who
offended it. While Sinn Féin campaigned for the expulsion

of 'human rights abusers' from the police, the IRA (like all the loyalist organisations) was beating young men with baseball bats, shooting them in the legs, or worse.

Those who spoke out against such activities were often denounced as anti-republican, or even anti-peace-process. Robert McCartney's sisters could not be denounced as either. These were five ordinary women – a nurse, a mature student, a teacher, a teaching assistant, a sandwich bar manager – from the same Short Strand streets as the men they believed killed their brother. Two of the five were Sinn Féin voters, as was Robert himself. What they were demanding, indeed, echoed some of the most often repeated Sinn Féin demands through the long years of political talks: justice and openness.

Sinn Féin responded with a mixture of evasion, denial and, in the case of one comment by Martin McGuinness, what sounded like very thinly veiled threats against the sisters. The sisters persevered. As their campaign attracted international attention – most worryingly, for the Republican Movement, from the USA – the IRA grew more desperate. At one point they visited the McCartneys and offered to shoot their brother's killers, an offer which the horrified sisters refused.

Then, on 28 July, came the IRA statement committing its members henceforth to exclusively peaceful means. There were many who saw this as an admission of the damage caused by the McCartney sisters' campaign. Certainly no one before them had brought the hidden reality of peace-process Belfast to the international gaze. In the past, however, IRA statements have been the equivalent of an 'erase' button, wiping the record clean for crimes committed before the statement was made. It remains to be seen how this latest IRA statement affects the investigation into the murder of Robert McCartney. Although the organisation claims to have expelled three of its members, the only two men to have been charged so far in relation to the murder were accepted onto the IRA wing of the prison where they were awaiting trial. (Both were recently released on bail.) Besides, the sisters insist at least three more men were involved in the killing itself, as many as a dozen in the subsequent clean-up. The IRA, they say, is still protecting them, still intimidating witnesses.

In the meantime the sisters have received hate mail and even death threats. Long after the IRA statement, Bridgeen Hagans's home was attacked with bottles and stones. She and Paula McCartney say they are being forced out of Short Strand.

As for Magennis's bar, it is now closed: a reminder of what didn't change after the first IRA ceasefire. International prizes are all very well, but the greatest reward for courage shown by the sisters of Robert McCartney would be for the change this time to be wholehearted and lasting.

Cicero Magazine, October 2005

D. I. O.

In recent days our towns and cities have witnessed racist attacks, homophobic attacks and violent assaults on the elderly, in addition to our familiar, but no less unpalatable, diet of vicious sectarianism and paramilitary beatings. (The paramilitaries, dear help them, are so busy nowadays it's a wonder they ever found time to fight their war.)

Like a great many people, I am outraged by these attacks. Like a great many people, I have found myself in the wake of them wondering what I can do. It is tempting to do nothing, other than mutter about our politicians, or simply despair. Though while we are on the subject of our politicians – and despair – why is it that none of them appear able to speak out against all violence, without distinction or equivocation?

I am not a well-organised person. I am endlessly 'busy' – it seems to be a law these days – and still fail to achieve a fraction of what I set out to. My energy and my outrage are all too easily dissipated. I wouldn't have the first idea how to start a campaign.

I mean, after mulling over the racist attacks in south Belfast for three days (in which time nine people had been intimidated out of their homes in Carrick and one man savagely beaten in Derry), this is the best I could come up with: on a day to be decided I would set up a small table in front of the City Hall, with an A4 notebook, an inkpad and rubber stamp. On the first page of the notebook I would write:

'We are people of Belfast. Attack one of us, you attack us all.'

Then I would invite anyone who lived in Belfast to sign, regardless of where they were born, or how long they had been here. (For that is the beautiful thing about a city, you don't have to qualify for citizenship: you live in it, you are of it.) And I would invite anyone in Carrick, or Derry, or any other city, town, village – street, even – with a table and an A4 notebook to do the same: 'We are people of X. Attack one of us, you attack us all.'

I even had a name for this date-to-be-decided. Do It Ourselves Day.

After all, I asked myself, what was the worst that could happen? I could feel lonely in front of City Hall for a few hours and a handful of others could feel lonely in Derry, or Carrick, or wherever. And the best that might happen? Well, maybe the racists, bigots, homophobes and senior-citizen-bashers would be left feeling a little lonelier by the time we all packed up our A4 files and went home.

But, then, that's not how campaigns really get started. Is it?

Oh, and the rubber stamp? Cheaper than badges. And faster: stamp the hand as it signs. One word: Person. Because whatever we look like; however old we are; wherever – or whether – we worship; whoever we choose to love, vote for, or cheer on at football; we are each no less than that.

Belfast Telegraph, July 2004

Love poetry, the RUC and me

When I was seventeen I fell in love for the fortieth or fiftieth time. It was a Saturday night in May. Earlier that day I had been to Windsor Park in Belfast to see Northern Ireland perform their annual feat of losing to England in the British Championship. The match kicked off at 3 p.m. I had been in the pub since 11 a.m. I was wearing a Northern Ireland jersey and at one point on the way from the bar to the ground I borrowed an Ulster flag from a friend and wrapped it round my shoulders. Supporting Northern Ireland has always been a peculiarly Protestant pastime.

This might have been the year Northern Ireland lost 0-2, or the year they lost 1-5. Anyway they lost, like I said, like they almost always did.

I was still drunk when I arrived home from the game at half-past five. I went to bed and slept the sleep of the teenage Northern Ireland fan, deep and disgruntled. My mother woke me at seven o'clock. My friends were at the front door. There was a disco on that night in a church hall on the Malone Road, a prosperous Belfast suburb about a mile and a half from our estate. This was 1979. The Troubles had been going on for ten years and there was little nightlife left in Belfast. My friends and I rarely ventured into the city centre after dark, but spent our weekend nights in the house of whosoever parents had gone out for the evening; drinking, playing cards, talking big. Sometimes we had girlfriends and then we would turn the lights out and love-bites would be painstakingly exchanged. The girls we went out with were all from our area. By the time I was seventeen every boy had been out with just about every girl at one time or another. My friends and I were always promising ourselves that some day soon we were going to find girls from other parts of town. A disco on the Malone Road was the sort of thing we dreamed of. Sitting up in bed that May evening, I could smell the Brut all the way from the front door.

I was in a bad mood. Northern Ireland had lost, as we all knew they would, even as we were in the pub singing about beating England, and now we were going to get drunk again, persuading ourselves tonight would be the night, and we would leave the disco without speaking to any Malone Road girls, never mind dancing with them. As we all in our hearts knew we would.

I don't know what motivated me to get out of bed in the end. Perhaps the same thing that motivated me to go to Windsor Park match after lost match.

So I got up and went with my friends and we got drunk again on tins of beer along the way and we left the disco without dancing with any girls. For once, though, we did have an excuse. A fight had broken out between some of our crowd and boys from another housing estate who had come to the Malone Road with the same intentions as us. Nothing serious, but the caretaker switched off the music anyway and called the police. Two grey Land Rovers were parked across the gates of the church as we all piled out and uniformed RUC men scanned the faces for known trouble-makers.

It was by now a little after eleven o'clock. The last bus from the city centre had already passed. My friends and I had a thirty- or forty-minute walk home. The shortest route would take us through the estate of the rival gang: Protestants, like us, though on a night such as this that scarcely mattered. A rumour went round that the police were cautioning and taking home anyone who appeared drunk. (Everyone there was under the legal drinking age.) A caution seemed to me a small price to pay for avoiding a hiding. I lay down on the tarmac in front of the church, among the feet of the teenagers still milling around, of the Malone Road parents come to collect their sons and daughters, trying to appear as drunk as possible.

The police ignored me. My friends ignored me. I lay where I was. I may not have been completely legless, but I was still drunk after all. I closed my eyes and when I opened them the world's most beautiful girl was peering down at me. From the ground I said to no one in particular, 'That's the girl I love,' and the girl smiled, becoming even more beautiful, and that was it, my heart was lost.

A few days later another girl came up to me in school and handed me a telephone number. It belonged to the girl I had seen outside the disco. It turned out she went to the same school as me. How had I not seen her before? Well, it was a big school, over two thousand pupils, and the girl, M, had only recently moved there from another school. And then too I was in the sixth year and she was just fourteen.

M was also Catholic. Or, at least, she had been baptised a Catholic. That is, I think she had been baptised; she was pretty casual about religion, pretty sceptical for a fourteen-year-old. It would improve the story, I know, if I was to say she was the first Catholic I had ever met. In fact, when I was a child religious integration was not unusual in Belfast, especially in the newer housing estates like the one I had grown up in. Many of our near neighbours had been Catholic; my on-off best friend (like all kids we fell out and made up on a regular basis) was Catholic. Besides, in my own family there were rural Catholic cousins. This too was not unusual. You did not have to go very far back in the history of many families, Protestant and Catholic, to find evidence of inter-marriage. Hormones, I find, make poor bigots.

Standing in the school corridor, clutching M's number, my own hormones were in a riot. She may not have been the first Catholic I ever met, but she was the first one (actually, the first girl *period*) who had ever asked me to call her.

I called, we met up and were together almost four years.

Of course there was one very important reason why M could adopt a relaxed, even irreverent attitude towards religion. Her family was well-off. The street where they lived was the Malone Road in concentrate, so exclusive that it was closed to through traffic. When a house went up for sale, it was said, residents would meet to vet prospective buyers. They were not concerned about religion, but *tone*.

In my own estate, a decade into the Troubles, many of our Catholic neighbours had moved out, some openly intimidated, others not caring to live with constant tension. They were replaced in many cases by Protestants from estates whose mixed make-up had run the other way. In the more densely populated parts of the city, tolerance was being squeezed out. There was barely room to question what this was all about.

There was so much room where M lived we could meet in the garden without being seen from the house. We could meet *in* the house and not be discovered. Though three years younger than me, she questioned everything as a matter of course. She mocked the extremes of Ulster loyalism and Irish republicanism in a way I had not heard before. She was scathing about anyone who simply went along with the crowd. Over a period of months I stopped going along with the crowd I had been with the night I first saw her. (I could never quite bring myself to stop going along to Northern Ireland matches, though from then on I steered clear of the Kop end, with its Ulster flags and sectarian chants.) My new friends were people who cared more about the Clash than either of Ulster's bloody causes.

I began to write. Love poetry mostly. I had thought about writing before I met M, but it was not something I would have spoken about openly where I lived. M was deeply unimpressed by my first efforts. Too lazy, she'd say, too sentimental, or sometimes, simply, too crap. And she was right. In writing as in politics I was in the habit of relying on other people's words. She taught me as well as any teacher.

I finished school at eighteen, but decided against going to university. (University to me meant England, moving away from home being half the attraction.) M still had three years of school left. I was waiting for her, I suppose. I got a job in a bookshop and made a failed attempt to start a poetry magazine called — don't ask me why — *The Alternative*

Duck. I almost never saw my friends from home now. Most of my new friends were at college in England. I was spending more and more time with M. Things were not always easy. Her father, worried about the intensity of our relationship, banned her from seeing me on more than one occasion. I would go off my food, sit up half the night drinking on my own.

I loved M with all my heart and I dreamed now and then of getting very far away from her.

Among the residents of her private street were a number of judges. Belfast being what Belfast was, these judges had round-the-clock police protection. One night, during one of M's father's bans, I was hanging about in the tree-lined street at the bottom of her long driveway when a police Land Rover pulled up. The policeman in the passenger seat asked me was I lost. I said I was waiting for my girlfriend. He asked me to point out her house and then asked if the people inside would vouch for me. I said yes, then immediately changed it to no. I explained about the ban, about how angry M's father would be if he discovered she was sneaking out to see me. The policeman looked at me doubtfully. He asked me to go to the rear of the Land Rover. There were another three RUC men in the back. They took down my name and address. One of them noticed I was carrying a jotter. He asked to see it. A jotter was a suspicious item. A jotter might contain details of judges' houses, the make and registration of their cars, the movement of police in and out of their remote-controlled gates. I handed the jotter over. The policeman flicked through the pages.

What are these? he asked me.

Poems, I said.

Yours?

I nodded. The policeman began to smile.

You're a poet, then, are you?

Sort of, I said.

Tell you what, another policeman said. You give us a poem, we'll give you a lift home.

I had missed the last bus again. The walk home had got no more pleasant in the time that I had known M. I climbed into the Land Rover.

Silence for the poet, someone said.

I mumbled a few lines of something so forgettable that I myself have forgotten the name of it.

Can't hear you in the front, the man in the passenger seat shouted. Speak up.

Stand up, the driver said.

Police Land Rovers are not made for standing in. I had to bend forward at the shoulders, my collarbone grazing the ceiling of the vehicle. A torch was shone on me.

That's better, the policemen agreed. Start again.

And so there, hunched in the back of a police Land Rover, in one of Belfast's most exclusive streets, I gave my first and only poetry reading, to an audience of five.

I read two poems and when I had finished the policemen applauded.

I don't know what they mean, one of them said, but they sounded all right.

In fact, they sounded terrible, as I had secretly suspected all my poems did. Still, I got my lift.

Some time after this I found myself again walking home very late from M's house. The received wisdom in those days was that if you did walk alone at night regularly you should vary your route. The route I had chosen this night was brightly lit much of the way. At one point, though, it skirted a road junction that led to Andersonstown in west Belfast. I was always relieved when I had negotiated this junction without mishap. This particular night as I approached I saw a lone car stopped on the Andersonstown side of the traffic lights. There were four men inside. I crossed the road in front of them, trying to look unconcerned. I had not gone fifty yards, however, when the lights changed and I heard the car come behind me. I ducked into the nearest driveway and walked quickly round the back of the house. I heard the car pull up and doors open. There were whispers, footsteps in the driveway. I stood close to the wall at the back of the house. At the bottom of the garden was a tall wooden fence and I was trying to calculate how easily I could scale it. The whispering stopped. After a time I heard the car doors shut again and the car move off. I waited another minute then walked back onto the street. The car was parked a hundred yards up the road, in the direction I had to walk. The instant I appeared its headlights came on and the engine started. I took off back towards M's street, a quarter of a mile distant. I hadn't a hope of outrunning the car, but as I drew level with the junction where I had first seen it, the car veered left and headed back towards Andersonstown. I stopped, looking after it, too relieved to be perplexed. It was only then that I saw, what the occupants of the car had already seen, a police Land Rover coming along the road ahead. I ran out to meet it, waving my arms.

I was driven home again. Over the police radio I heard that the mystery car had been stolen earlier in the night. It was later found abandoned and burned out. The police advised me not to go walking on my own at night in future, but I had already made that resolution.

It would be too neat – in fact it would be a big fat lie – to say this incident made me decide to leave Northern Ireland. It was only one of a number of scares I had in those years, but the urge to leave, and soon, was growing daily.

I knew if I went to England without M our relationship would not last. She had told me as much. If the truth were known, though, that too had begun to be an attraction. There were times when the atmosphere around her house could seem that bit too detached. In trying to cut myself off politically from my background, I had also cut myself off imaginatively. Perversely I had concluded that only by moving further away, to England, could I begin to reverse the process.

I left Belfast in October 1982. I was twenty-one. A year later I fell in love again, less dramatically, for the forty- or fifty-first time. I wrote a novel based on the estate where I grew up. M, who was by then at art college in London, read the novel and told me all the best lines were hers.

I haven't written another word of poetry since.

If I'm coming home late at night now I take a taxi.

.doc magazine, Stockholm, December 1997

The BBC made me a deconstructionist
(and called it macaroni)

If I had a great big medal I'd pin it on the person who dreamed up *Scene Around Six*. I'm sure the play on 'seen' was intentional. From that first syllable – sibilant – it was unmistakably of this place, where most of us are only ever an excited slip of the tongue away from the wrong end of the seen-saw. (And though Seen Around Six was grammatically correct, I half expected London to give us a collective slap: 'You *saw* it around six.') I don't remember news programmes before *SAS* came along, though I'm told they were much briefer. It must have seemed a gamble in 1968 to give Northern Ireland twenty minutes of nightly news to fill, but, credit where credit's due, Northern Ireland rose to the challenge, serving up, in *Scene Around Six*'s sixteen years, a constant diet of murder and mayhem for its cameras to feed off; feed us on.

It was on *Scene Around Six* I saw the car bomb explode. Maybe you saw it yourself. Yes, *that* one: a soldier in the foreground ducks just before the vehicle becomes less and more than the sum of its suddenly lethal parts. I saw worse things back then, on screen and off, but that seemed to me the perfect symbol of a society where everyday objects, and the lives they furnished, were no longer reliable.

It's probably too simplistic to say (but I'm a novelist, it won't stop me) all this fuelled my childhood desire for escapism: the Saturday Morning Club at the Majestic, the James Cagney Season on the BBC. I loved Cagney the tough-guy, of course, but I loved him too in *Yankee Doodle Dandy*, the bio-pic of George M. Cohan. I imagined myself the 'old timer' not recognised on the street as he left the White House with a medal for the song all the Doughboys were singing, 'Over There'.

Aged about seven, I tried writing my own song. I tried writing a lot of other things over the next twenty years before I tried a novel and, when that finally worked, tried another.

I was writing my third – was on the bus home from the pictures (*Lulu*, with Louise Brooks) – when I remembered the car bomb clip. I ran into the house and typed a passage. From then until the book was published, I didn't change a word, which is rare for me. As rare as deconstructing cars are these days, thank God; as rare as Sean Rafferty on our televisions, more's the pity.

The Living Air, BBC Publications, July 2005

It could be anyone

In one of his most celebrated stories Jorge Luis Borges tells how a simple lottery in the ancient city of Babylon is transformed by the introduction of unfavourable as well as favourable draws. For every thirty winners, there is one losing number, which carries with it a fine. Defaulters are sent to prison: the bigger the unpaid fine, the longer the sentence. Soon the lottery organisers have ceased to bother with the fines, publishing only their prison-term equivalents. As more and more unfavourable draws are introduced, the lottery starts to mimic, and eventually overtakes, the functions of judiciary and legislature. A sudden rise in fortune, an ignominious fall, a public execution, an unexpected erotic encounter, all are the luck of the draw. A company – The Company – is formed to manage the myriad draws necessary to control every aspect of public and private life. One of its first actions is to make the lottery free, universal and secret: henceforth whether you choose to enter or not, you are in. After the passage of centuries the workings of the Company have become so clandestine that the very existence of a Company is a matter of conjecture and life in Babylon is considered by many 'nothing else than an infinite game of chance'.

This brilliant closing sentence reanimates the cliché while giving it a paranoid twist. Has the author just exposed the arbitrary nature of all our carefully constructed systems, or hinted at a hidden hand behind the most random and outrageous occurrences?

Either way, as I sit here in Belfast in the late summer of 2005, Borges's story has never felt more relevant.

I begin this three days after a Sunday newspaper reported that the Provisional IRA have perfected the forgery of the new Northern Bank notes, introduced earlier this year to prevent the circulation of the £12 million in unused Northern Bank notes (out of a haul of £26.5 million) the same Provisional IRA stole last December. Except, of course, the Provisional IRA is no longer active, and besides, it did not steal any banknotes. Honest.

I begin this a few hours after the funeral of fifteen-year-old Thomas Devlin, stabbed to death as he walked home from buying sweets at a filling station on Belfast's Antrim Road: a seemingly motiveless attack, for which, it has gradually emerged, the UVF may have been responsible; has emerged and then receded again, as the suspects taken in for questioning are released without charge. This in turn recalls the aftermath of the murder, in January, of Robert McCartney, and the largely fruitless campaign by the victim's family for witnesses to come forward. The killers had notoriously removed film from the CCTV camera in Magennis's bar – had removed every speck of forensic evidence – before allowing the customers inside to leave. Those who did present themselves to the police simply refused to speak.

Although investigations are continuing into the murder of Thomas Devlin, and although two men have now been charged in the McCartney case, it is hard sometimes to shake the feeling that we are living in an age without agency. No one does anything; things just happen.

This is not just a law-and-order issue, it is also an epistemological one: what can we say with confidence that we know about the society we live in? And the doubts it raises may be undermining something more fundamental than a political process. What's more, its effects don't stop at the Northern Irish border.

The Small World Theory, or Six Degrees of Separation, draws inspiration from a 1929 story, 'Chains', by the Hungarian satirist Frigyes Karinthy, who is himself not separated by much – historically, geographically, temperamentally or even alphabetically – from Franz Kafka, and therefore, Kafka being a presence in all Borges's work, from the writer of the 'Lottery in Babylon':

'There were certain stone lions, there was a sacred latrine called Qaphqa, there were fissures in a dusty aqueduct which, according to general opinion, *led to the Company*; malignant or benevolent persons deposited information in these places.'

Events of the past few months have highlighted the possibility that there are far fewer than six degrees separating every one of us living in Ireland from paramilitary money and influence.

There is something *Qaphqa*-esque – I choose the spelling carefully – about the name Passage West. It was in this Cork

suburb in February that a man was discovered feeding hand-
fuls of sterling into a bonfire in his back garden. That same
day another man was arrested as he stepped off a train in
Dublin's Heuston Station with a Daz washing-powder box
filled with cash. Back in Cork, gardaí raided the Farran
home of Ted Cunningham, managing director of the
Chesterton Finance loan company, and discovered £2.3
million in a compost bin. They warned anyone else who had
come into large amounts of cash recently to report it to the
authorities. Hours later a man walked into a garda station
with a bag containing more than £150,000.

More arrests and seizures followed, from Offaly to
Dundalk, like a thread unravelling the length of the island
and – if I can marry two metaphors and put one in a suit
for the occasion – as far up the body politic as Phil Flynn,
close associate, on the one hand, of Taoiseach Bertie Ahern,
and advisor, on the other, to Sinn Féin, of which he is a
former president. Flynn resigned as non-executive director
of the Bank of Scotland in Ireland after it emerged that he
was also non-executive director of Chesterton Finance. He
flatly rejected accusations of involvement – by him or by
Chesterton – in money laundering and later, more pointed
accusations made under parliamentary privilege by the
Unionist Lord Laird about Flynn's relationship with two
alleged IRA leaders, Brian Keenan and Thomas 'Slab'
Murphy.

All the same, for a short time on the cusp of spring the
papers were full of revelations about IRA criminal activity
and the crossover, in personnel and funds, with Sinn Féin:
the Republican Movement, as it often referred to itself, was
indeed indivisible. There were the millions – possibly bil-
lions – invested in properties here and across the water;

there were the sympathetic accountants, solicitors, people with inside information on areas earmarked for rezoning. There was the attempt to buy a bank in Bulgaria.

From Leinster House to the White House there was the sense, if not the actual sound, of welcome mats being lifted, doors slamming shut. Even those who thought they knew a thing or two, it seemed, didn't know the half of it.

Somewhere in the middle of this five men were jailed in Dublin for IRA membership, part of a gang caught in a van with fake garda uniforms, truncheons, CS gas and election posters for South Dublin Sinn Féin TD Aengus Ó Snodaigh. And somewhere in the middle of this – with ever more disturbing details about Robert McCartney's murder continuing to emerge – the Sinn Féin vote went up in the Meath by-election.

One month later, and two days into another election campaign, for Westminster this time, Gerry Adams, speaking, as he said, with the authority of his office as president of Sinn Féin, made an appeal to the leadership of the IRA: 'Can you take courageous initiatives which will achieve your aims by purely political and democratic activity?' Few in the media, or the British and Irish governments, deemed it appropriate to point out that only a few weeks before they were in agreement that Adams's authority proceeded from his Sinn Féin presidency and his seat on the IRA's Army Council. The gap had appeared again between the two; doors that had been shut were once more open. Stories of republican financial dealings did not disappear entirely, but they slipped off the front pages, out of some newspapers altogether.

On 28 July, the IRA responded to Gerry Adams's call with an order to dump arms. Three days later the business section of the *Sunday Independent* reported that, in the run-up to the IRA statement, businesses linked to Sinn Féin's director of finance, Des Mackin, had 'suddenly lodged up-to-date accounts'. Many of the businesses were cash businesses, many had deficits running into the millions, many had addresses in the Parnell Centre in Dublin and many were 'ultimately owned in the British Virgin Islands and controlled by well-known Belfast businessman Peter Curistan'. Peter Curistan is the founder of the Sheridan Group, which, besides being the developer of the Parnell Centre, is the largest private investor in Belfast's Odyssey Arena. (Odyssey must have seemed an apt name for an arena that was sold as a beacon for a city emerging from decades of conflict and was launched on the world with a speech by Bill Clinton.) The *Sunday Independent* quoted the auditors' reports on various of the companies: 'no system of control on which we could rely,' reads one; 'we are unable to establish whether proper books and records were kept,' reads another.

In 2004 Peter Curistan was awarded the Northern Irish Institute of Directors' Lunn Award for Excellence. I am not, any more than the *Sunday Independent* was, suggesting any wrongdoing. I am, though, genuinely amazed to learn that there are large amounts of poorly-accounted-for cash circulating so close to the surface of our economy and so close to one of our largest political parties. But, again, what do I know?

Travel up the Sydenham Road half a mile from the Odyssey, cross the Dee Street bridge and take a left into Mersey Street and you will soon find yourself at a new housing development named after one of Belfast's best-known, but, till recently, least acknowledged (I believe the term in tourism circles is 'under-exploited') writers, CS

Lewis. Sited in what was formerly one of the most densely populated – and almost exclusively Protestant – parts of the city, Lewis Square is both a major piece of redevelopment and a major piece of rebranding.

I confess I have already had a lot of sport with the idea of Lewis Square: 'Deceptively spacious built-in robes', etc. I confess too that I sit on a committee tasked with better exploiting the Lewis 'product' ahead of the release, this December, of *The Lion, The Witch and the Wardrobe*, which is to be marked with a gala screening in the MGM multiplex at – where else? – the Odyssey.

There is to be a new CS Lewis trail, centred on east Belfast, which will in all likelihood take tourists past one of the several branches of Philip Johnston and Company, principal selling agents for Lewis Square. Earlier this year the company's founder and managing director was charged with money laundering as part of an investigation into the activities of former UDA brigadier Jim Gray (aka Doris Day), himself arrested a few days earlier in a car containing thousands of pounds in cash. Council offices in County Down were also raided and planning applications examined. A Unionist election candidate was briefly questioned.

The 'Lottery' conceit must be qualified by the recognition that there is more than one Company operating in Borgesian Belfast. There is more than one Company operating in loyalist parts of the city; indeed it is the protracted and bloody feuding between companies that makes their activities so public. So public and occasionally so farcical. Another story in the press as I write this: four members of the UDA convicted of trying to 'tax' an undercover policeman posing as an ice-cream seller in Carrickfergus.

(Make that minus sixteen degrees of separation. You don't have to go out of your way to ensure that your — or your children's — money finds its way to the Company: they'll bring the means, jingling-jangling, to the end of your street.)

Then again, maybe all that is unusual about this incident is that the culprits — evidently lacking the self-protective instincts of the people who murdered Robert McCartney — were caught on camera. In his 2004 book *Colours: Ireland from Bomb to Boom*, the *Observer* columnist Henry McDonald likens west Belfast to a one-party state-within-a-state where anything from bootlegged vodka to mini shopping centres may be run by 'the Movement', providing it with an income from this part of the city alone of £20 million a year. (A recent *Sunday Times* report adds disposable razors, toothpaste and washing powder — Daz? — to the counterfeit commodities; bogus mortgage applications to the financial services provided.) 'Sicily Without the Sun' is McDonald's term for it and he attributes the near invisibility of all this activity to the republican movement's totalitarian grip on the community.

He also draws attention to the activities of the IRA in the border areas, where it has profited hugely — and individual IRA leaders have profited hugely — from the smuggling of diesel fuel. (Cue those Flatt and Scruggs' banjos: 'Come and listen to a story 'bout a lad named Slab...') For diesel to be smuggled, diesel must first be 'washed', an innocuous term for a process that produces a waste so toxic that, McDonald claims, the Provisionals came within a whisker of poisoning the entire water supply of County Louth in the spring of last year. Add to this their alleged involvement in the illegal dumping of household waste, a growth industry since the introduction of bin charges in the South, and a picture emerges of an organisation dedicated to the removal of the border, profiting from its existence, while jeopardising the environment of the island whose integrity is its ostensible raison d'être. It is a picture as blackly comic as that McDonald paints of a Sinn Féin health minister (Bairbre de Brun) encouraging healthier lifestyles, while the IRA stole millions of pounds' worth of cigarettes for resale in working-class areas of Belfast.

Sinn Féin would deny any connection between it and these matters, as it continues to deny any link between them and the IRA; it would no doubt point to its manifesto: 'We are committed to the principle of sustainable development. We believe that all economic activity and policy decisions should be environmentally proofed to ensure no needless damage is inflicted to an island environment already under severe pressure from unnecessary pollution and inefficient waste management strategies.'

Borges would say, 'There is nothing more contaminated with fiction than the history of the company.'

If the forensic clean-up after the murder of Robert McCartney stands as one metaphor for the paramilitaries' attempt to control reality – what we can say with confidence we know – the IRA statement, as a genre, surely stands as another.

The first says something happened here, but no one did it. The second says we did do it, but *it* was not what you thought it was at the time.

IRA statements, or at least the negotiations that create the conditions for them, are, as I have written elsewhere, like an erase function – *revise* function might be better. They turn events into non-events.

In the wake of the 28 July statement, the question has to be asked: what will become now of the investigations into the Northern Bank robbery? Will the killing of Robert McCartney be retrospectively 'legitimised', as happened with the killing of Garda Jerry McCabe, whose killers' release became part of the Sinn Féin negotiations? And what will happen to the investigation into the possible UVF involvement in the murder of Thomas Devlin if, as rumoured, that organisation 'responds positively' to IRA decommissioning? Already, this bloody summer now ending, there have been suggestions that the police have been standing by, or have been instructed to stand by, while the UVF pursues its latest feud with the smaller LVF, in the hope that, having wiped out its rival, the UVF, like the IRA, fades into the background; or at least, the black-economy-ground.

Certainly the UVF has nothing to learn from republicans about the contamination of history. At the end of Cherryville Street in east Belfast is one of the new gardens of remembrance that are becoming such a feature of the post-Troubles city. Standing side by side in this one are two granite memorials, the first to the men of the area who died in the Great War, the second to men, some with no connection to the area at all, who died in our own not-so-great war. This second memorial includes the names of Wesley Somerville and Harris Boyle, who lost their lives taking those of three members of the Miami Showband.

'The indirect lie,' notes Borges, 'is also encouraged.'

In a conflict in which there were no winners — it's official — all parties get to write their own histories, paint them on walls, carve them in stone. Forget contamination, we are on the verge of a full-blown epidemic.

Or is that, to use the words with which Bertie Ahern greeted the 28 July statement, on the verge of something 'momentous, historic and unprecedented'?

The organisation that six months ago was being described by government ministers as the most sophisticated criminal enterprise in the world has apparently ceased operations overnight. Things continue to happen. Every now and then it is proved that someone has done them. In Dublin the City Council calls for an end to the intimidation of the family of Joseph Rafferty, shot dead in April as he left his flat. Sinn Féin say they support the family, but appear to be alone in thinking that Joseph Rafferty's killer is not a member of the IRA. Meanwhile the party prepares for the next Irish general election. The signs are the vote will continue to rise. I think of Borges again, not the 'Lottery' this time, but 'The Immortal'. How does it go? 'We accept reality easily, perhaps because we suspect nothing is real.' I lift down my copy of *Labyrinths* to check. Not 'suspect', 'intuit'. And then I notice the next line: 'What do you know of the *Odyssey*?'

As I sit here in my house, bought from an estate agent who has subsequently been charged with money laundering, I ask myself what do any of us know of anything?

About an hour after typing that last question mark I walk out onto the main road near my house and there, above the estate agent's window, where the mauve and red of Philip Johnston and Company should be, is a new colour scheme, a new name and a logo that on closer inspection represents a terrace of rooftops, but on first glance looks like nothing so much as a jagged line through past associations. Two days later the local free paper lands on the doorstep with confirmation: 'Estate agent caught up in laundering scandal sells firm.' (And yes, part of me is disappointed it doesn't say 'company'.) The new owners admit they paid 'a substantial sum in anyone's language', before concluding, 'We believe the rebrand will give the public confidence.' And do you know what? They are probably right.

Irish Pages, autumn 2005

Never-ending stories

It pains me to say this, a mere twelve weeks in, but I'm sick of it already. Not the Peace – God, no – but the Question: 'What are you going to write about now?' I have lost count of the times I have been asked this since the IRA announced its ceasefire on 31 August and the UVF, the UFF – the whole magician's-hatful of loyalist terror groups – followed suit in mid-October. Enough times certainly for me to have stopped using my stock response to enquiries from London: 'I don't know, what have people been writing about there all this time? And how *does* an Aga work?' (OK, so *almost* stopped using.) Reductive – stupid even – to characterise all English writing as Aga-sagas? No more so than it is to term everything that has come out of Northern Ireland in the past twenty-five years as 'Troubles writing', dependent for its very existence on the continuation of violence.

I admit that it came as some surprise to me to learn that writing fiction set in Northern Ireland had somehow been easing the passage into print all these years. I was, it's true, the object of one fellow student's envy while studying for an MA in Creative Writing at the University of East Anglia ('God, you're so *lucky* coming from Belfast'), though no more so than another student who, being northern *English* and by imputation working class, was also considered to have had his 'story' handed to him on a plate; and in practical terms the Troubles dividend remained elusive.

My first attempt at a full-length work of fiction was a screenplay, written when I was twenty-two. It was a pretty lousy attempt. Not that the agent I sent it to would have known that. The manuscript was returned to me within the week, only the cover letter having been read. It was 1983, less than two years after the Maze hunger strikes, a matter of months after Gerry Adams was elected MP for west Belfast; the supergrass trials were at their height, the New Ireland Forum had met for the first time in Dublin. Bernard MacLaverty's *Cal* had just come out.

'Northern Ireland has been done,' the agent said.

Publishers have in my experience generally been uncomfortable with Northern Ireland except in certain very particular genres. (Though some might say that publishers would be happy if *all* novels were set within a dozen tube stops of their London offices.) Flying into Belfast International Airport last year I found those preferred genres on prominent display. The local interest section at the book stand in the arrivals hall was overwhelmingly stocked with titles like *Provo* and *Contact*. Thrillers and true-life adventure, Ulster-style; books written, for the most part, by authors from outside Northern Ireland, offered to visitors almost by way of introductory guides. It was, it seemed to me, as though we had taken to projecting out the image projected onto us.

The confusion of Northern Irish *subject matter* with Northern Irish writing has not been helped, in the main, by literary critics and academics. Robert McLiam Wilson's second novel, *Manfred's Pain*, charted the final days in the life of an elderly Jew living in London. If for no other reason than that it confirmed the potential of *Ripley Bogle*, Wilson's hugely successful debut, *Manfred's Pain* would be a significant work in the history of recent Northern Irish writing. It is, however, routinely overlooked by commentators concerned with the past twenty-five years here. The author's current work-in-progress, *OTG*, his first to be set entirely in his native Belfast, will no doubt be received in some quarters as a late- (or even *post-*) Troubles novel. Yet to treat the work in this way, concentrating only on those books which include recognisably 'Northern Irish' material, is to ignore the thematic developments across the three novels, the development too of the author's distinctive moral philosophy. It might even be argued that in its treatment of the second world war, its engagement with the greater violence of the twentieth century, *Manfred's Pain* sheds as much light as any book on the effects of Northern Ireland's own violence on the psyche of its younger writers.

This failure to make imaginative connections extends beyond the study and consumption of literature. The complacency with which Northern Ireland in general has been regarded in the rest of Great Britain and Ireland has become more, not less marked since the end of August. Northern Ireland is seen essentially as a Northern Irish problem. By virtue of their proximity, and the inability always to contain the violence, the countries with whom we share these islands have had an interest in what has been going on here, but they have nothing to learn from it, no questions to ask of themselves. The vexed issue of Who We Are, for instance, is most often rendered a straight choice between two unassailably secure national identities, Irish and British. It is as though we have been talking to ourselves all this time.

I would not for a minute suggest that the problems of Northern Ireland should be as immediate to the people of Dublin or Durham as they are to the people of Down, but to dismiss them as entirely unrelated, the squabbles of an alien and benighted people, smacks of either arrogance or folly.

Earlier this year I read at the writers' union in Bucharest. Despite the language difficulty, the discussion which followed the reading was a revelation to me. The audience's responses did not focus on the surface particulars of the novel's setting, but on the underlying themes, applying them to their own experience. But why should I have been surprised? This, surely, is the purpose of all literature, that it communicates outside the specifics of the time and place of its setting, establishing a dialogue with its readers.

It is this kind of dialogue that a significant number of writers here (like a significant number of writers elsewhere in Britain and Ireland, I make no claims to our uniqueness) have been working to establish in recent times. But say some of us were to decide at a future date that we wanted to look again at the years of violence, what of it? Where does this notion come from anyway, that once a conflict ends it is closed once and for all to writers? Try applying it to the literature of the rest of Britain and Ireland this century. Kiss goodbye to the *Sword of Honour* trilogy, kiss goodbye to *Empire of the Sun*; kiss goodbye to O'Casey's 'Dublin plays', kiss goodbye to 'Easter 1916' ('a terrible beauty is born' and all); kiss goodbye to a significant chunk of Radio 4's weekly output.

The truth of the matter, as the Belfast critic Damian Smyth recently pointed out, is that cultural time and political time are not synchronised. Politics often lag behind ideas that have begun to take hold in the public imagination. Artists rarely initiate these ideas, though they may pick up on and amplify them. (The ceasefires were not announced into a void. It might even be said that the ceasefires occurred because the demand for them was there and increasingly making itself heard.) By the same token, it can take many years for a society to work through the events that have occurred in it, or even properly to understand them. And all the while new situations are arising.

I returned to Belfast in March, after some time in Manchester, and rented a terraced house just south of the city centre. To the right of the end of my street stands a row of cod-Georgian townhouses, to the left the slant-roofed church of one of Protestantism's legion sects. The townhouses and the church are exactly contemporaneous, built to replace earlier versions of themselves destroyed when the local police station (the gap behind the corrugated iron fence next to the church) was demolished by a bomb abandoned in a bus. The bus-bomb itself is only one of the many stories-from-the-Troubles; even now some intrepid director might be approaching Keanu Reeves to play the lead. (Don't worry about the accent, Keanu, it didn't stop Mickey Rourke.) It is doubtful, though, whether the aftermath of the blast would attract much in the way of outside interest.

Eight years on a new police station is being built, across the road from the old one, though 'police station' scarcely does justice to the scale of the construction. This, according to rumour, was to be a holding station for terrorist suspects; more than that, it was to be Super Station, practically bomb-proof. (There were rumours too of Japanese officials flying in to observe its design. Is there something the people of Tokyo ought to know?) The object of intense local opposition at the planning stage, the unfinished station is now the area's biggest joke: it will become a mall, some say, a Troubles theme park, say others; it is to be a nightclub complete with white-noise room. Or maybe it will survive into peace time as it is, putting other, smaller stations out of business, like so many corner shops when Aldi comes to town. The fact is no one knows, yet this phase of uncertainty is as important to understand as the one which preceded it, as the one which will in time succeed it. For the peace process is not an end in itself (though as the saying goes here, no one can process peace like we can process peace); it is a stage along the way to somewhere else equally provisional.

Northern Ireland can never be said to have been done, any more than the Republic of Ireland, England, Scotland or Wales can be. I am thirty-three, still termed a young writer, but already there are people beginning to write whose perspective on living here, living through the same events that I have lived through, differs radically from mine. Perhaps the word 'process', divorced from its current constant companion, holds the key to this whole question of what comes next. Process – the inevitability of change – is the simple experience of living. Messy and entirely human, here as anywhere, process is a story without an end.

The Sunday Times, December 1994

Traffic

traffic: vehicles, pedestrians, etc. (collectively), using a thoroughfare; similar movement at sea or in the air; the transportation of goods and people on a railway, air or sea route, etc.; the goods or people transported along a route...dealings or communication between groups or individuals. [From a Romance language...origin obscure.] *(Chambers Dictionary)*

I write, as I read, in no small part to feel less alone in the world. For much of the time this involves me sitting in a room in Belfast by myself. At the beginning of June 2000, however, the British Council invited me to join the Literature Express, a train running, by the least direct route imaginable, from Lisbon to Berlin (where the idea had originated) with one hundred and six European writers on board. There would be public readings and talks at stops along the way and in between times there would be hours, days, seven whole weeks, to discover what if anything connected us all.

By the end of the sixth week, having crossed twelve land borders, I knew one hundred and six people by sight, ninety-five by name. I knew – from frequent repetition and keeping company with writers from the Balkans – that *Sláinte*, the Irish toast, meant small elephant in Macedonian.

Midway through the seventh week, on the afternoon of Wednesday the twelfth of July, I stepped out of the Metropol Hotel in the centre of Warsaw and attempted to walk across a busy intersection, the rondo Dmowskiego. It was not a smart thing to do. I had ignored the pedestrian subway almost immediately in front of the hotel; ignored too the brace of policemen standing by their patrol car out on the roundabout.

The policemen did not ignore me. They watched me for some moments hop and shimmy between cars and trams. Then one of them blew his whistle, bringing traffic to a halt, and waved me over. The policeman spoke very good English. I explained to him that the last time I used the underpass I had been confused and come up on the wrong side of the street. He explained to me (in his very good English) that he was going to fine me anyway, for jay-walking.

'After all,' he said. 'If I came to your country and walked in the middle of the road, I would expect to be fined too, wouldn't I?'

In fact, if he'd come to my country that Wednesday afternoon he would have seen tens of thousands of people walking in the middle of the roads. The twelfth of July is the day when the Protestant Orange Order commemorates a battle fought on the River Boyne, in the Irish midlands, in the year 1690. Parades – and opposition to them – have been a feature of political life where I live more or less ever since.

I didn't tell the policeman this, any more than I told him that there was a Peugeot 206 hanging from the fifteenth floor of the Metropol Hotel behind him. I didn't want a bigger fine for being cheeky.

We had arrived in Warsaw from Minsk, in Minsk from Moscow, covering hundreds and hundreds and hundreds of miles of the Great European Plain. It's hard not to be awed by such distances; hard not to be fired by the sense of possibility they inspire.

Three days before I went jaywalking, I had lain on my bed in Minsk watching, on BBC World, a bottleneck of marchers and riot police in the narrow country lanes at Drumcree parish church near the Northern Irish town of Portadown. The marchers were members of the Orange Order who wanted to parade through a Catholic district. The Catholic residents said there was another road the marchers could have used. Either way, the distances involved could be measured in hundreds of yards. The same dispute had flared in each of the past four summers. In previous years unrest had spread to many parts of Northern Ireland. Cars were hijacked and burned as roadblocks. In Belfast, shops shut early, bars and restaurants didn't even bother to open. For a week, sometimes longer, in the sunniest month of the year, people would come home from work and lock their doors for the night.

On my last day in Minsk, BBC World showed a deserted Belfast city centre; it showed a bus with no passengers and no driver. It was the bus that ran past my house.

I phoned my wife from Warsaw. I asked her how things were. Not so bad, she said. At least our local video store was still open. My wife had walked down there the night before to hire a film. Some women were gathered, chatting on the footpath, by the exit from a roundabout. A few had children with them, one had a baby-buggy. The roads, all this time, were empty, but as my wife left the video store, a solitary car drove towards the roundabout. It indicated to turn off at the exit where the women were standing.

And then, said my wife, the women rushed it. They kicked the doors, thumped the windows, bounced on the bonnet.

The women were a sort of roving roadblock. Between them, they very nearly succeeded in bringing the car to a halt.

I was reading *War and Peace* on the train from Moscow to Minsk, from Minsk to Warsaw. (Actually, I had been reading the thing for most of the last six weeks.) Much of the journey had followed the retreat of Napoleon's army in 1812. Vyazma, Smolensk, Orsha.... I looked out the window recalling descriptions of chaotic flight: 'from all sides, like the roar of the sea, was heard the rattle of wheels, the tramp of feet, and incessant shouts of anger and abuse'.

Tolstoy often refers to the wars in the first fifteen years of the nineteenth century, in the wake of the French Revolution, as a 'movement of peoples from west to east and a counter-movement from east to west'. The Battle of the Boyne was part of a much smaller movement of peoples at the tail end of the seventeenth century. The victor, William of Orange, was Dutch and (oddly for a man who has inspired generations of Protestants) carried the blessing of the Pope. The loser, James II, had been deposed by William (his son-in-law) as king of England and had the active support of Louis XIV of France. The religious and political tensions which led to this particular battle in this particular place were already centuries old. It's commonplace to say that, in Ireland at any rate, the Battle of the Boyne did not bring them to an end. Then again, it's hard to know where any strand of history starts and finishes. So, instabilities in Louis XIV's France, caused in part by the cost of constant wars, were exacerbated during the long years of his son's reign and finally, in the reign of his grandson, Louis XVI, contributed to the overthrow of the monarchy, leaving the door open for Napoleon, and so on.

The comma is history's punctuation mark of choice.

From as early as I can remember I was excited by the thought that all roads must inevitably connect. The street outside my house connected with another street, which connected with another, which connected with the main road into the city centre. Here, a series of turns brought you to the ferry port from where you could be taken, by a specified sea-lane, to another port, another road leading out from it, and so on. Each road, however small or badly repaired, belonged to the worldwide union of traffic-bearers. Once you had set off there might be pauses, but there would be no full stops.

I had never heard then of Kaliningrad.

In 1945 the East Prussian city of Königsberg fell to the advancing Red Army. The remaining German population was driven out, westward. Tens of thousands of people were forcibly moved from other, eastern parts of the Soviet Union and settled in their place. The city was renamed Kaliningrad and closed to the outside world.

I visited Kaliningrad en route to Moscow. I found a bridge there with no road leading on and no road leading off. I spent a long time looking at this bridge, as though it was a sculpture, a concrete message. I took several photographs, the better to contemplate it when I left.

Due to a visa mix-up a Croatian writer, Jurica Pavicic, had to leave the train between Kaliningrad and Petersburg and return home to Split. Jurica and I had become firm friends. We shared a liking for football, PJ Harvey and for the work of self-proclaimed 'trafficker in climaxes and thrills and characterization and wonderful dialogue and suspense and confrontations', Kurt Vonnegut Jr. Jurica planned to join the train again for the last leg of the journey, from Warsaw to Berlin. It seemed unlikely to me he would make it. The journey overland from Split took more than a day. It took half a day to explain. And yet in Warsaw on the night of the twelfth of July I took a photograph with Jurica in it, against the backdrop of the Hotel Metropol where Peugeot, in an effort to persuade more people to buy their cars, had suspended a 206 from the fifteenth floor. The real subject of the photograph, though, was a section of redbrick wall next to Jurica on the left of the frame. The wall – maybe twelve feet by ten – stands a few yards to the east of the rondo Dmowskiego. It is illuminated by three red carriage lamps, of the sort you would find outside a country inn. Into the centre of this wall a granite plaque has been set commemorating one hundred and two Polish citizens who, in 1944, were rounded up, marched here and massacred by the Nazis.

One hundred and two. More or less the number of writers we had been moving around Europe with for the last month and a half.

Numbers can numb, which is why literature will sometimes succeed where simple documentary fails in conveying the horror of war. Literature particularises, its mathematics is unitary: one plus one plus one plus one…Think of Edgar Derby, in Vonnegut's *Slaughterhouse 5*, shot by firing squad in the ruins of Dresden for taking a teapot. Think of the factory lad Pierre sees awaiting execution in *War and Peace*, in the last moments of life adjusting the knot of the blindfold so that it isn't pressing into the back of his head.

The ultimate end of propaganda, on the other hand, is to reduce human beings to the one sentence, word even, for which they can be murdered. It stresses the differences between groups of people as though they were so many freestanding bridges.

In Kaliningrad, I met a man whose great-great-grandmother was a cousin of Tolstoy's wife, Sophia. He drew me a diagram, more road map than family tree: there was a road leading off to Milan, another leading in from Scotland, from where there are roads into my own family.

Maybe it's time we stopped thinking about roots and thought instead about the *routes* by which we have been arrived at. We are walking *bus terminals* for history.

traffic: 'from a Romance language…origin obscure'. Let's hear it for all our obscure origins.

The movement of peoples that provided Tolstoy with the subject of *War and Peace* began to grind to a halt on Sunday, 18 June 1815 on the battlefield at Waterloo, not far from Brussels.

One hundred and eighty-five years later, to the day, fifty-eight would-be immigrants from China's Fujian province were found dead in the back of the lorry smuggling them into Dover.

At the time they were commencing their journey, I was travelling in the opposite direction, from Brussels to Dortmund on the Literature Express.

*

One autumn Sunday in Belfast, two months after leaving the train in Berlin, I was trying to write an essay about my experiences. It just wasn't coming together. My wife and I had people staying. I heard talk of a drive along the coast. The sun was shining. I switched off the computer and tagged along.

We drove out of the city – past the roundabout where my wife saw the car being attacked – and down the Ards Peninsula to Mount Stewart, formerly the summer home of the Marquises and Marchionesses of Londonderry, now managed by the National Trust. We walked in the gardens and then, the day having grown colder, went on a guided tour of the house. My head was still full of what I had been trying to write; I didn't take in a lot of what was said in the first two rooms we saw. In the third room, however, the dining room, the guide pointed out twenty-two upholstered chairs ranged round the walls. These chairs, she explained, were from the Congress of Vienna, which had been meeting in 1815 when Napoleon escaped from Elba and launched the campaign that ended at Waterloo. One of the Londonderry family, Lord Castlereagh, had attended the Congress as British foreign secretary. He brought the chairs back as souvenirs.

They are there in the empty dining room at Mount Stewart as I sit, miles from Vienna, miles from Warsaw and Minsk and Moscow, from my friends in Kaliningrad and Split, from Fujian province on the far side of the landmass that includes what we call Europe, telling you this, trying to make the connection.

Radio 3, June 2002

Homelands
(Presented at the 3rd Dublin International Writers'
Festival, September 1993)

It seems appropriate when discussing homelands to begin
by remembering a writer who is spending today, as he has
spent the past more than fifteen hundred days, in the most
grotesque form of exile imaginable, the there-and-not-there
existence imposed on him by an Iranian death sentence. I
am speaking of course of Salman Rushdie, a writer who has
always had much to say on the subject of homelands. Here,
for instance, in his third novel, *Shame*, he interjects himself
into his narrative to speculate on the meaning of belonging:

'To explain why we become attached to our birthplaces,
we pretend we are trees and speak of roots. Look under
your feet. You will not find gnarled growths sprouting
through the soles. Roots, I sometimes think, are a conserva-
tive myth designed to keep us in our places.'

I owe a great debt to Salman Rushdie. It was after reading his novel about the birth of India, *Midnight's Children*, hard on the heels of John Dos Passos's *USA*, that I decided that the novel was the form most appropriate to the subject of Northern Ireland. It was only later when I had published my own first novel, while living in England, and had returned to Belfast to live and write that I discovered that a number of my contemporaries had likewise been inspired by his work. His stories of lives lived in one place, dominated by thoughts of somewhere else – his characters' attempts to negotiate the space in between – struck a chord with us growing up in Northern Ireland's split-personality state. He was, in fact, we used to say, and not entirely joking, the most important *Irish* writer of his generation.

Shame in particular, his 'novel of leavetaking' from the East as he calls it, published the year after I first went to live in England, spoke to those of us who had shared at one time or another his emigrant condition: the irresistible impetus to leave, the unresolved concern for the country, the homeland, left behind.

Leaving Northern Ireland as I did in the year after the Maze Hunger Strike, leaving it in part because of the Hunger Strike – still to my mind among the most collectively shameful (as well as personally terrifying) episodes in the last twenty-five years of Irish and for that matter British history – leaving, as I say, when I did, why I did, I had moved to East Anglia, to Norwich, as far away from Belfast as it was possible to get in Britain without falling into the sea. I had already had an unappetising taste of emigrant communities while visiting relatives in Canada, visits which included the bizarre experience of marching alongside an

Orange parade in lily-wilting heat through crowds of bemused Toronto shoppers.

I had rarely seen the Sash worn with such belligerent pride.

A happy coincidence of the move to Norwich therefore was that there appeared to be only one other person there from Belfast. I knew that's where he was from because he had very helpfully been re-christened Belfast Dave. When eventually we met he informed me that from the instant I arrived I had been known – to everyone else if not to my face – as Irish Glenn. So it is we often find ourselves, willy-nilly, defined by the very thing we are trying to leave behind.

The reasons for emigration, of course, are many and complex. Some emigrants have no desire to leave the homeland at all and hang on for dear life to its memories and rituals. The Orange marchers I mentioned are only an extreme example. I think of the men in Ciaran Carson's poem 'The Exiles' Club' meeting in the Wollongong Bar, somewhere in Australia, engaged in the Joycean task of reconstructing the Falls Road of their youth, right down to the contents of Paddy Lavery's pawnshop. Even Salman Rushdie, the enthusiastic exile, cannot always trust in the effectiveness of his escape. The East remains a part of the world to which, he says, he is still attached, if only by elastic bands. And of course if you force an elastic band beyond a certain point, there is either an irrevocable break, or an inevitable return.

It is interesting that in *Shame* Rushdie's most strongly expressed attachment to his homeland comes when he recalls his anger on hearing of the sale of his childhood home in Bombay. This seems to me to point to something, perhaps glaringly obvious, about the emigrant's sense of homeland: it is inherently nostalgic, arrested as it is at the moment of his or her departure.

Of course I have been talking up to now of homeland as an essentially individual longing. (I am tempted here to substitute the word *heart*land for homeland, both in recognition of the strongly emotional nature of the longing and for its often expressed desire to be lost once more in the bosom of one's own people.) I would suggest, however, that there is something fundamentally nostalgic about even the collective expression of the word. This in turn is not to ignore the sustaining potential of thoughts of homeland for people who have been displaced or who are otherwise suffering discrimination because of their race, their religion or their nationality, nor to deny the need for spatial as well as legal refuges from persecution.

Again I am sure this has been mentioned many times already in the past two days, but the theme of this festival has been made even more pertinent in the weeks since its announcement by the signing of the peace accord between Israel and the PLO.

For its joint commitment to a demilitarisation and for its restoration of certain fundamental rights to people who have been denied them for almost half a century, the accord is clearly to be welcomed.

It is equally clear, however, that the accord still faces serious opposition, both from those Israelis who see any concession as a threat to the security of their state – the Jewish homeland which the Holocaust had made such an urgent necessity – and from those Palestinians who see it as a dilution of the homeland they were deprived of when the Israelis claimed theirs. This is much more than a territorial dispute. What we are faced with are two competing versions of homeland written onto the same geographical location. Worse still, in each version the homeland can also be read as *holy* land (centred on Jerusalem), with all that term's attendant baggage of god-given rights and destiny fulfilled in soil.

Quite apart from a desire to see an end to the fighting in the Middle East, I find myself drawn to the example of the Israelis and the Palestinians both as a writer – the idea of competing narratives – and as a native of Northern Ireland. In fact, the parallels between the two conflicts are so well developed in the minds of most Northern Irish people as to have passed over into their own country's sectarian iconography. In various parts of Catholic west Belfast, therefore, you will come across murals depicting the PLO and the IRA as comrades in arms (and indeed throughout the 1970s the local press regularly carried reports of republicans receiving training in camps in Lebanon); Protestants, meanwhile, have traditionally admired the Israelis for their uncompromising response to what they both regarded as terrorism. In my teens many Protestants wore (and perhaps many still wear) the Star of David, each of its six points being said to represent one of the counties of Northern Ireland. For a time my local member of parliament in south Belfast was a man, a minister of the church, who claimed, apparently in all seriousness, that the Ulster Protestants were descendants of the lost tribe of Israel and as such had an unshakable claim to their six-county state.

One Saturday morning in 1981 five men with a very different idea of the arithmetic of homeland walked into a community centre not far from my parents' house and shot the MP, the Rev Robert Bradford, dead, along with the caretaker Ken Campbell, who alternated with my brother opening the centre on Saturdays.

Again we have two fundamentalist readings of the same territory. It is at one and the same time the country that once promised a Protestant parliament for a Protestant people and the Fourth Green Field, the piece needed to complete the picture of a unified Gaelic nation. The dispute hinges, as these disputed readings often do, on a single hard-to-interpret line, the border. Or perhaps saying a single line is an oversimplification, for borders, as everyone knows, are a recurrent motif in Northern Ireland. Or perhaps again the larger line is like one of those titles that only come to the writer after the book is complete, a culmination of the themes running through the text rather than their precursor. For long before there was a border, Northern Ireland was border country.

The state of Northern Ireland itself is of course, in historical terms, relatively young. Even in human terms it is not that old. My grandmother at eighty-two is ten years older. But then, my grandmother at eighty-two has seen the Soviet Union come and go, has seen, to pick a place at random, the territory of Alsace-Lorraine translated back and forth between the German and French on no fewer than three occasions in her lifetime. She has, in fact, seen the formation of more new countries than I can practically enumerate here and the collapse of as many old ones.

Nor do I mean to be flippant in saying this. If the fact of our own mortality is the hardest lesson that we as human beings have to learn, then the acceptance of the impermanency of institutions we have been brought up to think of as defining who we are cannot lag far behind.

Wanting to suggest something of this belief in countries

as shaping forces — as *characters* — in our lives, I called my own second novel *Fat Lad*, an acronym I was taught at primary school to remember the six counties of Northern Ireland by: Fermanagh Antrim Tyrone Londonderry (for it was a Protestant primary school) Armagh and Down. What we weren't taught until much later was that the Fat Lad could so easily have been *A* Lad, pure and simple, slimmed down to two-thirds his actual size by the exclusion of the potentially unbalancing (because predominantly Catholic) counties of Fermanagh and Tyrone. There is an arbitrariness here, or rather a degree of calculation, that undermines faith in the current arrangement.

Maybe it is this more than any other factor that explains the appeal of Salman Rushdie to me and my Northern Irish contemporaries, his recognition of countries as willed (or imposed) fictions, like all fictions susceptible to editing and revision.

Fat Lad was in part an exploration of how people live with such contingency, of the psychological impacts of political decisions which redefine, however subtly, their country's meaning, if I can call it that. Let me give you an example from my own life. When I was eleven the British government announced a referendum, quickly dubbed the Border Poll, in which the people of Northern Ireland were asked to vote for or against staying in the United Kingdom. I was petrified. Never mind that nationalist leaders were advising their supporters not to take part in what they saw as a mere rubber-stamping of the unionist veto: for days beforehand I could barely sleep. I cried with relief when the result came through. This was undoubtedly, in part, a political reaction: even at eleven, even in a mildly unionist household like the one I was brought up in (my lullaby was 'Kevin

Barry'), I knew by heart all the arguments in favour of the
link with Britain. There was at the same time, though, a
much more irrational element to the reaction. Pull away the
border and it would have seemed to me then as though the
bottom had dropped out not just of the country, but of all
my notions of order.

Or let me, if I may, give you another, more oblique
example. My father is a sheet-metal worker by trade and for
many years made railings in his spare time. He had a car, a
Vauxhall station wagon in which to ferry the finished railings
about. It was by far the biggest car on our street, possibly in
our neighbourhood. It was a bus, practically, and could fit our
entire under-10s football team inside. (The word 'dismay' to
me is the look on the faces of opposing teams seeing us roll
up to their pavilion in my father's Vauxhall. That car was a
two-goal start.) One night in autumn 1971 we were stopped
by paratroops in the centre of Belfast on our way from
Aldergrove airport where we had been picking up a Canadian
uncle. We were ordered out and made to stand against the
window of Marks & Spencer; my mother, my father, the
Canadian uncle and me. My father chatted, as my father always
did (and does – this is a man who walks sideways so as not to
miss anyone he knows going in the same direction only
slower). The paratroops weren't having it. They pulled the film
from my uncle's camera. There went London, there went Paris.
Next, they emptied the glove compartment and the boot of
the big station wagon. Next, they took off the door panels and
unbolted the seats and set them on the pavement.

These were *our* soldiers. This was our *car* – our family on
wheels – and there it was for all the world to see on the
pavement outside Marks & Spencer. It had not even
occurred to me till then that you could do that to a car. My
first engineering lesson and it was a lesson in deconstruc-

tion. Even after the Paras had put it back together I never quite trusted that car in the same way, but sat by the door from then on with my hand near the button, ready to bail out the instant it threatened to fall apart again.

While it is rare that the terms of the contract between the people and the state are presented in the stark terms of the Border Poll, they are nevertheless restated daily in a myriad of small, and not-so-small, ways. And if the state acts outside the limits of its power, or outside the people's expectations of it, then one of two things will happen; either the state loses its legitimacy in the eyes of the citizen, or, equally likely, it provokes a crisis in the citizen's sense of self. Though apparently contradictory, both responses can have the same result. It seems to me that what are called, appropriately enough, *disturbances* when they reach the street cannot be divorced from these psychological upheavals.

As a writer, especially as a writer who has spent a lot of time living in England, I find myself confronted by two major problems when trying to deal with this situation as it relates to Northern Ireland. The first is personal, or perhaps ethical, in that the lives of the people I am writing about closely resemble those of people whom I grew up among. The second is theoretical or political: in focusing on Northern Ireland as an imperfect fiction, how do I avoid giving the impression that I am trying to write it out of existence? So far as the personal question is concerned, perhaps this is something writers never resolve. We draw heavily on the communities – families even – which nurtured us, and even when we write out of a desire to inform, in the broadest sense, it is hard sometimes not to feel, in the narrowest sense, like an informer.

As to the political question, it has always seemed to me that what writing about Northern Ireland could do, and by writing I suppose I am talking about the novel, was find ways of portraying the events there not as existing in a vacuum, but in their historical, political, geographical, even *geological* context; as a part of the broader currents of European and world history.

At the same time I repeat over and over to myself a formula that I think is necessary for anyone who would seek to effect change there, namely that two things can be simultaneously wrong; or put another way, by drawing attention to the frailties of one system of belief, you do not automatically espouse its opposite. Indeed, even to think in terms of opposites in a place like Northern Ireland is to perpetuate the problem. Militant republicanism is not the opposite of diehard loyalism, the union of Northern Ireland with Great Britain is not the opposite of a United Ireland. Nor for that matter, to take an example from elswhere in the world, is an Orthodox Serbia, a Catholic Croatia and an ethnically segregated Bosnia the opposite of Yugoslavia.

It is, however, one of the most depressing aspects of the current turmoil in Europe that so often change can only be envisaged as a return to a previous – or even to a supposedly original – state.

This picks up on something I said earlier, about the idea of homeland, even in its collective expression, being inherently nostalgic. The nostalgia I had in mind was what I would call the nostalgia of nationalism. Homeland, as it is increasingly used in our present political climate, presupposes a nation, or rather a People; homeland, more and more, connotes exclusive possession and at its most extreme adopts the deadly rhetoric of racial purity. There is at the moment, I am told, one Serbian politician who claims the

Serbs have descended, not from the lost tribe of Israel, but from *another planet*. A joke on his part – I think – but one which merely takes to its logical conclusion the extreme nationalist's dream of the uncontaminated people. This yearning for pristine states is, I would suggest, ultimately infantile in nature. (It is worth remembering homeland's synonyms: fatherland, mother country.) It is a desire for the familiar, for the uncomplicated state. As such it is anti-organic. People move, have always moved, over the earth's surface. The *land* moves over the earth's surface. The present configuration is as fleeting as a snapshot; a billion years from now the earth will hardly recognise itself. Preposterous of course to think in terms of such a timescale, but not half as preposterous, or as vain, as the argument of absolute proprietorship.

No man, as the saying *ought* to go, can set a limit on the progress of a continental drift.

Nor is the west of Europe free from this charge of exclusivity, as the recent resurgence of overtly racist groups in Germany, France, Britain and Italy makes abundantly clear. Yet even leaving this worrying trend aside it seems that we are unable to expand our concept of homeland without explicitly excluding other groups of people. So the lifting of internal borders within the European community has been accompanied by a strengthening of its eastern and southern frontiers. Buffer zones are established, holding countries for refugees; immigrants are classed with terrorists and drug traffickers as suitable targets for surveillance.

During the time that I was thinking about this paper I began to get confused, the way you sometimes do looking at the same words for extended periods, about the precise meaning of the terms I was using. I thought I had better go right back to basics and start again with succinct definitions. People. Nation. Race. All the big concepts that are used to describe and divide us. The more I looked, though, the more elusive agreed definitions seemed to become. The one defining characteristic of a people that did recur was a shared belief in a common history (shared language apparently being an optional extra). So I set to work trying to figure out from that who my people were. My family. Obviously. But who else after that? The people in the part of Belfast where I grew up? Well, accepting the very particular family history we could not possibly share, yes, them too; in fact, by the same reasoning *all* the people of Belfast. What then of the people in the rest of Northern Ireland – the rest of Ireland, south and north? Didn't the common history extend to them? Well, a little more tenuously perhaps, but yes, to them too. And to Britain? Yes. And beyond that…And beyond that…And beyond that…?

I started to grow very excited; each time I considered drawing a line under this idea of a common history there seemed to be an equally strong reason why I should extend it just a little bit further. I was reminded of one of those moments of insight you have, waking suddenly in the middle of the night with a thought that seems to have come to you perfectly formed, irrefutable in its simplicity. Of course, these thoughts rarely survive exposure to the corrosive light of day and more often than not turn to nonsense in our mouths when we try to communicate them.

But anyway.

One night a couple of years ago I woke with what I thought was some kind of wonderful Zeno's paradox in my head, only instead of motion it was difference between people that it proved was impossible. And it went like this: difference between peoples cannot exist because the closer you approach any notional dividing line, the more, not less, alike people actually become. (In the same way borders are least necessary in border country, well away from the respective – that word again – heartlands.) And this would hold no matter how far you journeyed throughout the world. You would never perceive change occurring, all you would experience would be a continuum.

As I say, my sense of well-being at this night-thought did not last much past breakfast, but it has come back to me more than once lately watching the news and thinking with dismay that in our ever more minute distinctions of ourselves as a People we are losing sight of everyone else as human beings.

(Again Bosnia, but Belfast too, and Brick Lane in London.)

We all have need at some time in our lives of the security that a sense of belonging to a community can give; few of us are entirely free of emotional attachment to the places where we were born or grew up. The retreat into homelands as a political model, however, into national or racial self-interest obscures the connections between us, prohibiting the development of a critique that might indeed radically alter the distribution of power and resources to the benefit of all people, and deferring the moment when we can truly enter into an accommodation one with the other.

New Writing 4, 1995

Out of myself

It is Friday night in Brussels. I am in *Bozar* at the launch of a festival – *Grand Hotel Europe* – reading a piece I wrote for a British Council book on identity. The piece begins 'I am one of the three hundred and twenty million people living in the states of Europe' and ends, 'Correction, I am the only person.' It is a reminder to myself as much as anyone that the mathematics of identity, like the mathematics of literature, is unitary: one plus one plus one...

There are ten writers reading at the launch. It almost midnight when we leave *Bozar*. In my head the lights have already dimmed on the *o*, *z*. 'Bar?' I say.

It is Friday – another Friday – afternoon in Bristol. I am in a bookshop. My wife and I have flown in from Belfast for the weekend (we're doing the world alphabetically). Friends, family, have been telling us we look tired: 'A break would do you good: take you out of yourself.'

We have checked into our hotel, reserved our table for dinner. We have even arranged massages. (My back these days feels more like a knotted stick.) We have everything except books. Our holiday habit: buy when you arrive; buy pretty much on impulse. Stepping into this shop I spotted the new book by Orhan Pamuk. Its title, *Snow*, is the title of the poem by Louis MacNeice that first got me writing. I take it to the till.

It is Wednesday afternoon in Belfast. I am on a bus. It has been raining since Wednesday morning. Bristol already feels like more than half a week ago. I am not sleeping: work worries. I can feel the knots reforming along my spine. I open my book for the first time since Sunday. Ka, the hero, is a blocked poet, returned to Turkey from Germany. He has come to Kars, near the Russian border, during a snowstorm, which has cut the town off. Bad things are happening. A man has been shot in a café where Ka was having coffee. An acquaintance has been arrested and beaten. Ka, when I find him on Wednesday afternoon, has been waylaid in a train station by three youths who interrogate him about his beliefs.

And suddenly he sees – really sees – one snowflake out of the millions that are falling. And just as suddenly he feels a poem start to form, the first in years. 'Although he had yet to hear the words,' says Pamuk, 'he knew that it was already written... Ka's heart rejoiced. He told the three youths that he was in a hurry and left the deserted, filthy station.'

I look up. I am in Ballyhackamore. This is my stop. I nearly didn't get back in time from Kars. I hurry home in the Belfast rain. Like Ka's, my heart is rejoicing.

It is the wee small hours of the morning after the Friday night in Brussels. I am still in that bar, with friends from the British Council. The talk turns from *Grand Hotel Europe* to a festival they are organising. Titles are being bandied about and out of my mouth, before I have half considered it, comes 'Out of Ourselves'. It is where reading (and writing) takes us: out of ourselves and into other lives. It is a communion as silent as snow, a reminder to all us units of identity: you might be the only person, but you are not alone.

'Out of Ourselves' festival brochure, Brussels, 2005

Christmas 1994

So this particular Christmas I'm thinking of, I'm in Lisburn, south of Belfast, out of love, trying to finish a novel. I have a flat on the first and second floors of a house on Bachelors Walk. (On Friday evenings when I stop work I drink gin and practise looking wry about this, but end up looking only like I have been drinking gin.) To my left fifty yards is the train station. Around the corner to the right, towards the town centre, is Antrim Street, where, in what is now Apollo Window Blinds, my father was born. His younger brother, my Uncle Edmund, earned pocket money riding on a pig's back from the station to the market square, pursued, as intended, by the rest of the herd; his elder sister's husband, my late Uncle Jamesie, an army bantam-weight champion, used to take on all-comers every Friday evening at the corner of Antrim Street and Bow Street. These

189

stories, which I have heard many times, have a different res-
onance now looking down onto the places where they happened.

This particular Christmas, the past seems ever present.

My desk is by the living room window which looks
directly into the first-floor offices of a personal finance
company across the street. Personal finance. From where I
sit writing I am granted a view of the ins and outs of the
whole business. Last thing on Friday and first thing on
Monday, women with pushchairs arrive at the company's
street door. I see them press the buzzer. One flight up, I see
them being observed on the monitor above the reception
desk. A professional pause/An anxious moment. I lose the
women and their pushchairs for a few instants in the inte-
rior stairwell then see them appear again – waist and pram
handle up – across the reception desk. They always leave
hurriedly. There are, after all, a finite number of shopping
days and Christmas is nothing if not insistent.

Next door to the finance company, Comet Electric's
Christmas promotion is in full swing. One morning I watch
forty-two Danny Kayes mouth the story of the Ugly
Duckling, in perfect sync, and I remember Christmases
mapped out in viewing schedules: *Holiday Inn, It's A Wonderful
Life, Son of Pale Face.* Then forty-two square eyes blink and
everywhere cartoon Titans clash. Mega Christmas, Danny,
wherever you are.

Since the end of November a truck bearing a giant sandwich board has passed my window once every fifteen
minutes on its endless circuit of the town's one-way system.
Santa says shop here, buy this. And this and this. He is
tailed every so often by a pair of army Land Rovers. Always
a pair. Each time I catch sight of one out of the corner of

my eye I begin instinctively to count under my breath. I never get beyond six before the second Land Rover passes too. (Months later, in Manchester, I have a dream in which I count and count and the second Land Rover doesn't show. I wake feeling sick with panic.) Lisburn is a garrison town. Thiepval Barracks, Army HQ, is less than five hundred yards from my flat, left off the junction of Bachelors Walk and Bridge Street. In the late summer of 1969 I saw tanks – not scout cars or armoured personnel carriers, proper tanks – on Antrim Street where before almost the only car I can remember having seen was the custom-built red sports car belonging to Davy Jones, Lisburn's celebrated (and at the time almost septuagenarian) dwarf, who for half-a-crown, my father told me, would sit on an upturned pint glass. Fair play to you Davy, I think now, though then I was scared of him, how many half-crowns are there in a red sports car?

Shortly after I moved into Bachelors Walk, one end of Market Street was flattened by a van bomb. There have been new and permanent roadblocks erected since then. The one-way system now has only one way in and one way out as well as one way round. Even so, I have written passages of my novel in a café in the nearby shopping mall, evacuated while the army dealt with suspect cars and packages in Bachelors Walk. These hours in the café are rare neighbourly affairs. I see the people from the personal finance company and we rise above our mistrust of each other's professions to say, yes, this is all an inconvenience, but then again you can't be too careful. And you can't. Really. Market Street is only the latest reminder. A wreath of plastic flowers on a lamppost just along from the swimming pool, across the road from Bow Street Mall, marks the spot where one summer evening six soldiers who had taken part in a charity fun run were killed when a booby trap bomb exploded under their car, and the Robin's Nest, facing the station, the pub where I have recently been organising poetry and prose readings, is also the pub from which two soldiers were once lured to a non-existent party in Belfast's university area and shot dead.

And there have been many other killings, loyalist as well as republican. There have been shootings and stabbings and even fatal beatings in town centre bars. It requires more than Christmas ceasefires to take the chill off memories like these. And then one morning, the week before Christmas, I'm writing as usual when for no reason I can think of I look up from the page and down into the street just as a foot patrol turns into Bachelors Walk from Antrim Street. As the last soldier passes beneath my window I notice that he has a sprig of mistletoe hanging from the webbing of his helmet. I write this down, quickly, thinking to make something of it later. (I am reminded of the festive pig, an old Belfast recipe: take one Saracen Armoured Car – pig, in Troubles' argot – wrap around with tinsel and garnish with inflatable antlers. 'Please note,' I say when I tell this joke, because that's what I have always made of the practice, 'this recipe is traditionally half-baked.') I look again, the soldier is looking up at me. The inverted V of mistletoe is like the projection of a rifle-sight, the berry a bead drawn on his forehead. And in that moment I don't want to write, I want to kiss him. Mouth on mouth, my head his head, singular and plural. This is what union means. This is unity. These are the useful meanings. Entangle our lives with our tongues, so that whatever is done to one of us is done to us all.

And the second he has gone I look at the words webbing and mistletoe in my notebook, and I don't know what to make of them after all.

Until this Christmas, back in Belfast, hearing the talk of peace grow every day more assured, and I feel the want of it in the hinges of my jaw; mouth open, waiting.

Signals, 1997

Afterword

New, shorter A–Z

A

Away. They have gone, you know.

B

Banknotes. And so have quite a lot of them.
But still. Favourite qualifier of British and Irish governments, usually followed by 'things are a lot better than they were X years ago'. Last heard some time between the disappearance of the banknotes and the 'they' of A.

C

Communities. One step forward – belated recognition that there are more than two communities here – two steps back – as witnessed by recent vicious attacks on the gay community, the Chinese community, the Polish community.

D

Davis to Healy who shoots.... And in a flash erases eighty years of Windsor Park nightmares. And where was I when the England net bulged? In the toilet.

E

ER2, The Exiles Return. Don't tell me I was in the toilet for that as well? No? You mean it still hasn't been aired?

F

Flags. Fewer and farther between than in the recent past, but your average Belfast street on your average rainy Tuesday could still give the Mall on Coronation Day or O'Connell Street last Easter weekend a run for their money.

G

George Best City Airport. So far joke-proof tribute. Only road-widening work scuppered earlier plan to rename the Westlink 'Bestlink' on the grounds that it was always blocked by four.

H

Hotels. We build them like we used to build ships. Then take the people who stay in them to see where we used to build the ships. New proposals for the Titanic Quarter will cut out the middle man: the shipyard will become a giant hotel.

I

Independent Commissions. Like other organisations beginning with *i* in years gone by these have proliferated of late. First came the Independent Commission for the Decommissioning of

Paramilitary Weapons, then the Independent Commission for Ceasefire Monitoring. Can only be wound up by the appointment of an Independent Commission for Independent Commission Decommissioning.

J

Juries. About to make a comeback here just as they come under threat in the rest of the UK. What will it take from us next, internment? Oh, right.

K

Kilrea. The new County Derry Bethlehem. Birthplace of Martin O'Neill, saviour of the Celtic-supporting nation.

L

Lewis, CS. Subject of recent 'Protestant cultural icons' mural. *Lewis, John.* Subject of repeated planning applications. Like we need more out-of-town superstores. Like we need more murals. More 'Protestant' or 'Catholic' anything.

M

Maze. Site of a proposed national sports stadium and conflict resolution centre. Presumably referees will have the option to send fractious players from one to the other.

N

Neck. What we have by the yard, with our conflict resolution centres, while our walls get higher and our politicians continue to talk the old talk of People and Territory.
n't. Sorry, dropped off 'have' earlier. (See 'Away'.)

O

Organs. Apparently Northern Irish people are more likely to donate theirs than people from any other part of the United Kingdom. The fact that the percentage willing to receive organs – 96% – is higher than that ready to give – 90% – should not in the circumstances be held against us.

P

PUP. Ever get the feeling you'd been sold one?
PSNI. Totally, totally unacceptable to Catholics, which accounts for the large numbers applying to join. Now has a Gaelic football team. Fair play to them. And the GAA, at long last.

Q

Queen's University. Home to the Seamus Heaney Centre (I teach there) and, soon, the Seamus Heaney Library. What are the odds that in the 2020 A–Z you will find the entire university under S?

R

Rankin, Paul. Restaurateur and celebrity chef. More than anyone has challenged the myth that Northern Irish men can't cook. And the myth that we all have cute accents.

S

Securocrats. Sinn Féin's Macavity. The question now is did Sinn Féin dream them up or did they dream up Sinn Féin?

T

Troubles. Sorry for them. Truly.

U

Ulster Scots. Like prose, it seems we had been speaking it all these years and didn't know it.

V

Vacuum, the, free newspaper. A beacon of wit and sanity and occasional silliness. (See 'Bestlink' gag above.) So guess whose funding that bastion of dimwittedness, insanity and perpetual silliness, Belfast City Council, has withdrawn?

W

Water charges. 'Say no to H^2O tax': the first cross-community graffiti since 'Help the RUC, beat yourself up'. Which reminds me, will there be a metre on the water cannon that disperses the H^2O rioters?

X

Quantity, in years, to be divided by 26.5 million to calculate how much better we should be feeling to be alive in 2006. (See 'But still' above.)

Y

'yes I said yes I will Yes'. Page apparently missing from the David Trimble Book of Helpful Quotations, bought at car boot sale by one IK Paisley. I'll pop it in the post, IK.

Z

Zadie Smith. Ours by marriage (to Cookstown poet and novelist Nick Laird). Who wants zeds when there's Zadie to be read?

June 2006